A LegenDerry Year

Edited by Garbhan Downey

Guildhall Press

First published in June 2014

Guildhall Press
Ráth Mór Business Park
Bligh's Lane
Derry BT48 0LZ
T: (028) 7136 4413 F: (028) 7137 2949
info@ghpress.com www.ghpress.com

The authors/photographers assert their moral rights in this work in accordance with the
Copyright, Designs and Patents Act 1998.

Design by Kevin Hippsley/Guildhall Press
Copyright © Garbhan Downey/Guildhall Press and various contributors.
ISBN: 978 1 906271 88 6

Cover photographs © Brendan McMenamin, Emmett McLaughlin, Martin McKeown,
John McDaid, Phil Cunningham, Bernard Ward, Stephen Boyle and Tom Heaney.

We gratefully acknowledge the financial support of the Arts Council of Northern Ireland
under its Annual Funding Programme.

A CIP record for this book is available from the British Library.

For Michael McGuinness (1935–2014)

Chairman of Guildhall Press and gentleman of culture.

Acknowledgements

This book would not have been possible without the support of the many dedicated photographers who contributed their work – and so many precious memories for the city – to this project. Unfortunately, space does not allow us to name everyone who contributed to the 5,000-picture archive we built up in the throes of this project. So, to all you who got in touch, please accept our eternal thanks. Your help is greatly appreciated.

A number of photographic experts, camerapersons and archivists worked closely with us, contributing to the book and/or advising us. Many thanks go to: Martin McKeown, Gavan Connolly, Emmett McLaughlin, Stephen Boyle, Lorcan Doherty, Tom Heaney, Michael Harkin, Brendan McMenamin, Bernard Ward, Robert Posluszny, Stephen Latimer, Keith Moore, Phil Gamble, Joe Boland, Jim McCafferty, William Cherry, Phil Cunningham, Jim Hughes, Nathaniel Harkin, Paul McGuckin, Andy Horsman, Kirsty Osborn, Jim Collins, Terry Coyle, Declan Sheehan, Harriet Purkis, Peter McKane, Anna Czajak, Andrew Monk, June Bradley, Deirdre Harte, Damian McClelland, John Boyle, Bertie Whiteside, Carol Cunningham, Dan Cullen, Pat Devine, John Gibson, Linda Heaney, Robert Quinn, Roisin Clifford, Simon Fallaha, James Cunningham, Joe McAllister, Seána Hippsley, Sara Roddy, Mickey Cooper, Matthew Greenall, Mark Nagurski, Willie Deery, Clare McCallion, Caroline Donnelly, Mark Lusby, John McDaid, Kevin McCallion, Brendan Grant, Clare Melarkey, Claire Lundy, Paddy Nash, Diane Greer, Conal McFeely, the McGuinness family, Charlie McMenamin and Frankie McMenamin.

A major debt of gratitude is due to those who contributed information, support and funding including: Martin Melarkey, Phil Redmond, Mike Doran, Kevin McCaul, William Allen, Una McNally, Declan Carlin, Culture Company, Portrait of a City, the Department of Culture, Arts & Leisure (DCAL), Department for Social Development (DSD), Ilex, Derry City Council, Creggan Enterprises, Echo Echo, CultureTech, Playhouse, Walled City Music Partnership, Cultúrlann Uí Chanáin, Waterside Theatre, Millennium Forum, Nerve Centre, U3A Camera Club, Eden Place Arts Centre, An Nua Productions and Greater Shantallow Community Arts.

To anyone we may have omitted to attribute or acknowledge, please be assured it was unintentional. We thank you also for your creative input and will endeavour to rectify our omission in any future editions.

Oonagh McGillion (in green top) prepares to drive the Derry City of Culture bid document to the judging panel in Liverpool in June 2010.

A LegenDerry Year

The images, words and stories captured by this book will tell their own story. It will not be the full story. For everyone involved in the year will have their own particular tales to tell and above all, memories to recount in later years, trying to put their selfies or souvenirs into context for those who were not there and, at times, to remind those who were.

It is what happened in Liverpool in 2008 during its time as the UK host for European Capital of Culture. It is what inspired the idea behind UK City of Culture. The title itself is only a mechanism to bring people together. It was, and still remains, simply a badge of authority that gives people an excuse to try something different.

Liverpool did it. Derry-Londonderry did it – and in so doing has set the stage for Hull to do it in 2017. To try something different. Above all, to remember the city's own culture. And use those cultures to work together for a better future. In Liverpool, we remembered the words of George Harrison: 'All things must pass.' In LegenDerry, Seamus Heaney put it better: 'Believe that a further shore is reachable from here.'

2013 was a great year, as this book illustrates. It should be remembered not as the end of anything but the beginning of something else. A stepping stone from a shared, if divided, past – toward a common future.

I would like to both praise and thank all those involved for delivering what was promised. Who could ask for more than that?

Phil Redmond
Chair, Independent Advisory Panel
UK City of Culture

A Tidal Wave of Culture

Derry-Londonderry-Doire has, for centuries, prided itself on being the cultural capital of these islands. It baffles its citizens that it's taken the rest of the planet until now to catch on to the fact.

To the wider world, this was a city best known as the home of Colmcille, of civil rights and Seamus Heaney – and of the finest Elizabethan walls in Europe. Those who knew a little more could perhaps tell you – prompted by our double Eurovision-winner Phil Coulter – about the 'music there in the Derry air'. And with a bit more nudging, they might also remember *Danny Boy*, Snow Patrol, The Undertones, Peter Cunnah or Nadine Coyle.

Dramatic types would, no doubt, have heard of Tony-winner Brian Friel, Hollywood star Roma Downey, the Field Day theatre company or the Oscar-nominated writer Dave Duggan. And those of an artistic temperament might speak with some authority on luminaries like two-time Turner Prize nominee Willie Doherty, or sculptors Eamonn O'Doherty and Maurice Harron.

But there were few indeed, outside northwest Ireland, who appreciated the full depth and breadth of the city's cultural and historical experience. Until now, that is.

Four stalwarts of the City of Culture Bid Team, pictured at Ebrington in 2010 (note – work still in progress on the Peace Bridge), during a visit by competition judges shortly after the city had been shortlisted for the title: Oonagh McGillion, Noelle McAlinden, Jennifer Neff and Claire Lundy. Aideen McGinley, Ilex CEO and bid organiser, can be seen in the background speaking to Phil Redmond, the chair of the judges, among others.

From the moment in July 2010, when Derry – population just 110,000 – was awarded the City of Culture title, there was a universal civic determination to share and showcase the city's complete and glorious tapestry. Inspired by the words of our patron poet, we began to believe in miracles again – chief among them the miracle of self-healing and self-revealing. So much so that by the time the programme for 2013 was published in October 2012, Derry was ready to host more than 500 jaw-dropping cultural events – from street exhibitions to global broadcasts.

Physically, too, the city had never been more prepared. Landmark buildings like St Columb's Cathedral and the Guildhall underwent major facelifts; our railway got a £50m upgrade; new lighting was installed across the city and along the historic walls; hundreds of businesses, shops and homes were powdered and painted; and the new riverbank walkways were scrubbed until they shone. And that's before you even consider the opening of the spectacular new Peace Bridge and the Ebrington site. Visiting journalists ran out of synonyms for 'transformation' and 'regeneration'.

The buy-in, both locally and internationally, was huge. Communities across the region embraced projects like the Music Promise and Portrait of a City, which – helped by City of Culture DSD capital funding and DCAL programme funding – in turn sparked a lasting legacy in the form of new neighbourhood cultural hubs such as the Hive Studio at Ráth Mór.

Word spread quickly outside the city, too. The exact statistics still aren't in yet, but it's safe to say in 2013, Derry enjoyed its highest number of tourists ever. By a country mile. During one event, Fleadh Cheoil na hÉireann in August, the city's population expanded to four times its normal size. And by the time the year was over, everyone, from the *New York Times* to the BBC, agreed that this was truly a cultural haven on earth.

Key to the success was the fact that no one individual or group ever owned, or attempted to own, the project. It was the property of the whole city and its people. As one wise organiser advised at the outset, it is amazing what can be accomplished when nobody looks for credit. But in this case, all credit goes to the city and its people, who ran the project as their own – and made it great – the minute the Department for Culture, Media and Sport threw them the ball.

This book tries – through the work of the city's finest photographers, and a few visitors besides – to provide some idea of the magnitude and magnificence of 2013. But just as 2013 could only realistically provide a snapshot of this city's 1,500-year heritage, so, too, this book can only provide a snapshot of a phenomenal year.

We have been forced to reduce an initial portfolio of more than 5,000 submitted photographs to just over 1,000 – and then somehow summarise 365 action-packed days and 560 events in just 272 pages. We were never going to cover all the key moments – there were just too many. So, we apologise in advance if, in parts, there is a feeling of merely scratching the surface.

The year 2013 was not perfect. Few would dispute it could have benefited from substantially more funding, more prep time and less red tape. But it was bigger and bolder and more beautiful than anyone could ever have imagined. And in spite of any flyspecks, the city's ambition – to explore its history, illuminate its talents, and tell its new story to the world – was achieved with endless style and relentless pride.

This book, today, helps tell that new story. It is a story of joyous celebration and it is a story of purposeful inquiry. Most importantly, it is the story of how a city embarked for a further shore on the far side of revenge. And which now docks there.

Garbhan Downey
Editor

Maurice Harron's new sculpture, 'Celebrate', at Ráth Mór was commissioned under the City of Culture Individual Artists programme.

The Bid Team flying the flag for Derry at the Nerve Centre in 2010.

Contents

The Run-In

Ebrington is a 26-acre former star fort, which served as a closed-off military barracks for 170 years before being restored as civic space in 2011 when it was reconnected directly into the city centre via the new Peace Bridge.

It is a perfect example of how Derry has spent the past two decades turning swords into ploughshares or, in this case, parade grounds into playgrounds.

And there is no doubt that the opening of the new, shared space, right on the river, in the heart of the city, was one of the key factors in making 2013 such a success. The site would host countless open-air concerts, community events, launches and fun-days; it became home to a giant pavilion (capacity 4,000), purpose-built for 2013; and its beautifully renovated Victorian buildings would house the first Turner Prize competition ever staged outside Britain.

Much has been written about Derry's superb campaign to become the first UK City of Culture: the themes; the breathtaking Snow Patrol/Seamus Heaney video; and the joy with which the July 15, 2010 announcement was received at the packed Guildhall. There was also the huge symbolism of the win – coming just weeks after the Bloody Sunday Tribunal findings were published – signalling a city experiencing a great renewal.

But it wasn't until 2012 that the citizens of Derry began to get a sense of just how big a deal the City of Culture year was likely to become. At the end of January that year a delegation from the city travelled to Dublin to lobby for the All-Ireland Fleadh to come to the North for the first time. They came home in triumph – and the event would prove the biggest ever staged on the island.

At the start of 2012, the TV producer and linchpin of Liverpool 08, Phil Redmond, visited Derry – along with the international panel that gave the city the award – to make sure preparations were on track. And by thunder, they were.

Then, the Ebrington factor began to kick in. Bronagh Gallagher officially opened the site with a barnstorming gig on Valentine's Day 2012, and on June 21, Jude Law emceed a massive 'Peace One Day' concert on the former parade ground. The event, which marked the official opening of the 2012 Olympic Festival, featured Pixie Lott (left), Imelda May, The Guillemots and Derry band The Wonder Villains. The London film producer Michael Hamlyn, a longtime friend of Derry, underwrote the ticket costs to give all 10,000 fans free entry to the concert.

The official City of Culture launch on October 25, 2012 also took place at Ebrington – followed by an evening reception a few hours later, 400 yards across the Peace Bridge in the City Hotel. A fleet of taxicabs, liveried with the new City of Culture logo, were presented on the square to special guests which included the Deputy First Minister Martin McGuinness and the 2013 mascot 'Oakey Dokes'!

A massive live-screen TV in Waterloo Place began counting down the days and hours until January 1. And just to give a taster of what was to come, in December 2012, the Field Day theatre company set up camp in the Playhouse for the first of their City of Culture performances. On this occasion, Oscar nominee Stephen Rea directed young Antrim dramatist Clare Dwyer Hogg's debut play 'Farewell' to rave reviews.

Summer showers can't dampen the spirits of these revellers watching Imelda May at the Peace One Day concert in Ebrington in June 2012 © Lorcan Doherty, courtesy Culture Company.

The expectant Imelda May. © Lorcan Doherty, courtesy Culture Company.

Stealing the show: The Wonder Villains. © Lorcan Doherty, courtesy Culture Company.

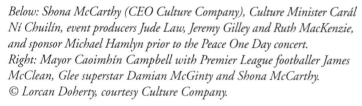

Below: Shona McCarthy (CEO Culture Company), Culture Minister Carál Ní Chuilín, event producers Jude Law, Jeremy Gilley and Ruth MacKenzie, and sponsor Michael Hamlyn prior to the Peace One Day concert.
Right: Mayor Caoimhín Campbell with Premier League footballer James McClean, Glee superstar Damian McGinty and Shona McCarthy.
© Lorcan Doherty, courtesy Culture Company.

13

It's an honour to be here in Derry. This is a fantastic city to host such an event and I hope it sends out a clear message. I am totally delighted to make the gesture.

Jude Law

Crowds at Ebrington for the Peace One Day concert.
© Lorcan Doherty, courtesy Culture Company.

Newton Faulkner.
© Emmett McLaughlin.

Damian McGinty with a couple of young fans.
© Lorcan Doherty, courtesy Culture Company.

Above: Cultural ambassadors Bronagh Gallagher and Paul Casey at the launch of the Hive Digital Studio and Cultural Hub at Ráth Mór. Right: Bronagh and her mum Maeve with Conal McFeely, Creggan Enterprises, and Paul McFadden, Leapfrog Communications, at the Hive opening in 2012. © Nathaniel Harkin.

Left: Digital guru Damien Randolph (Dee.ie) with Joe McAllister of Guildhall Press and Guildhall Press Chairman Michael McGuinness, author, historian, singer and footballer, at the opening of the Hive Studio in Ráth Mór. Right: Charlie Nash with Paul McCloskey and Eamonn O'Kane at the launch of the Ulster Elite Amateur Boxing Championships. © Martin McKeown.

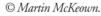

In November 2011, the Executive of Comhaltas Ceoltóirí Éireann arrived at the City Hotel to meet Derry civic leaders to discuss their bid to host the Fleadh. Included in the city delegation were Mark Durkan MP, Gearóid Ó hEára (Comhaltas), Mary O'Dwyer (Ilex), Shona McCarthy & Martin Bradley (Culture Company), Sharon O'Connor (Derry City Council), Catherine O'Connor (Derry Visitor & Convention Bureau), Odhran Dunne (DVCB), Philip Gilliland (Londonderry Chamber) and Garbhan Downey. © Tom Heaney.

Above: Culture Company CEO Shona McCarthy welcoming Field Day to the city in preparation for their productions in 2013. © Lorcan Doherty.

Top right: Culture Company Chairman Martin Bradley with UK City of Culture Chair Phil Redmond. © Tom Heaney.

Below & right: Eimear and Ryan McAllister enjoying the Painted Cow parade in Ebrington Square and Foyleside Shopping Centre in 2012. Courtesy Joe McAllister.

Walled City Music Partnership Executive Director Matthew Greenall takes a first look at the City of Culture programme at the launch event in 2012. Courtesy Culture Company.

Below: Culture volunteers at the programme launch in Ebrington in 2012. © Stephen Boyle.

www.cityofculture2013.com

Above & left: Deputy First Minister Martin McGuinness and Mayor Caoimhín Campbell with City of Culture mascot 'Oaky Dokes' and volunteers at the programme launch event at Ebrington in 2012. © Stephen Boyle.

Left & above: Culture volunteers distribute the programmes citywide, with staff at Ráth Mór in Creggan (including: Joan Murray, Danny Cassidy, Paul O'Connor, Geraldine Fitzpatrick, Carol Cunningham, Harry Crossan, Colette Stewart and Pavathi Subramanian). © Stephen Boyle.

A fleet of branded taxis is on hand to take volunteers to every outlying corner and community in the city to distribute programmes.

The City Hotel is emblazoned with projected images of Derry's cultural heritage to mark the programme launch. Below: A range of cultural events are held across the city centre to celebrate the release of the 2013 programme. © Stephen Boyle.

18

Above: The Wonder Villains. Below: MP for Foyle, Mark Durkan, speaks to the guests at the evening launch. © Stephen Boyle.

Above: Deputy First Minister Martin McGuinness addresses the assembled audience at the launch. © Stephen Boyle.

Below: Best Boy Grip entertains the crowd. © Stephen Boyle.

www.bestboygrip.co.uk

Guests at the evening event.

January

The Undertones – under the watchful eye of producer Frank Gallagher – headlining the Sons and Daughters concert. © William Cherry, courtesy Culture Company.

The first of the year's 140 'major' events would be the largest-ever tea dance staged in the city, held on January 5. It was hosted by Mayor Caoimhín Campbell at The Venue, a massive pavilion purpose built at Ebrington for 2013.

More than 1,000 ballroom dancers thronged into The Venue for the free event, to celebrate the city's long love affair with music and dance.

Elsewhere across the city:
• A Colmcille-themed exhibition of sculpture got underway at Eden Place Arts Centre;
• The Void Gallery unveiled a Candice Breitz video installation;
• The Playhouse launched its first production of the year – Seamas Keenan's 'Over the Wire' – to wide acclaim;
• The first of more than 20 international conferences kicked off at the University of Ulster's Magee Campus when MeCCSA opened the annual bash for top media academics; and,
• The Ulster Elite Boxing Championships was held.

The 'official' 2013 launch, however, came on January 20, with a huge concert at The Venue featuring the best of homegrown talent. This 'Sons and Daughters' event was compered by actors Jimmy Nesbitt and Amanda Burton, and was broadcast by the BBC. It included appearances by Snow Patrol, The Undertones, Nadine Coyle, The Divine Comedy, Paul Brady, Phil Coulter, Dana, Best Boy Grip, Ruth McGinley, Mairéad Carlin and Soak.

Carnival performers In Your Space at The Venue. © Gavin Connolly.

It's [The Venue] a beautiful place. I've been watching it being built from my bedroom window so it's good to be here now.

Kathleen Gamble, tea dancer

The inaugural tea dance at The Venue. Courtesy Culture Company.

Photography ©
Gavin Connolly.

SOUND OF THE CITY

Derry rings in the New Year with a concert at the Nerve Centre celebrating the best of local talent. There were performances from Triggerman, Our Krypton Son, John Deery & The Heads, Little Bear, Best Boy Grip, Intermission, Wyldling and Making Monsters.

Images courtesy Culture Company.

Above: Scene from 'Over the Wire' by Seamas Keenan at the Playhouse. © Gavin Connolly.

Top right: One of the first babies born in 2013 at Altnagelvin Hospital in the city receiving the 'Baby's Day Out' publication by Dog Ears, given to every baby born in 2013. © Lorcan Doherty.

Right: Author Adrian Kerr with Jenni Doherty (Guildhall Press) and Eamonn McCann at the launch of 'Free Derry: Protest and Resistance' (subsequent winner of the McCrea Literary Award) in the Museum of Free Derry. © Stephen Boyle.

Below: Homegrown talent Paul Casey, Bronagh Gallagher, and Paddy Nash & the Happy Enchiladas perform at the Millennium Forum. Courtesy the Forum.

Below right: Culture Minister Carál Ní Chuilín with Raymond McCartney MLA and Culture Company's Martin Melarkey speaking to artist/photographer Jim Collins during a visit to the Portrait of a City (POAC) project and Hive Studio at Ráth Mór. © Emmett McLaughlin.

Ulster Elite Boxing Championships featuring a range of Derry boxers, including champion Conor Coyle (St Joseph's, Derry) – pictured being congratulated by Derry Boxing Olympian (1972) Charlie Nash and Deputy First Minister Martin McGuinness – and Sean Magee (Ligoniel) and Kevin McIntyre (St Joseph's). © Lorcan Doherty and Martin McKeown, courtesy Culture Company.

Above: Snow Patrol with Derryman John McDaid on keyboard/vocals and cultural champion Gary Lightbody on guitar/vocals. Snow Patrol gifted their anthem 'Just Say Yes' for use as Derry's City of Culture campaign song. Below: A section of the crowd at the Sons and Daughters concert at The Venue.
© William Cherry, courtesy Culture Company.

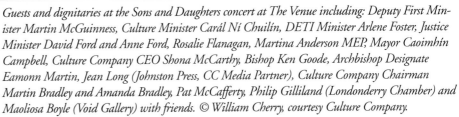

Guests and dignitaries at the Sons and Daughters concert at The Venue including: Deputy First Minister Martin McGuinness, Culture Minister Carál Ní Chuilín, DETI Minister Arlene Foster, Justice Minister David Ford and Anne Ford, Rosalie Flanagan, Martina Anderson MEP, Mayor Caoimhín Campbell, Culture Company CEO Shona McCarthy, Bishop Ken Goode, Archbishop Designate Eamonn Martin, Jean Long (Johnston Press, CC Media Partner), Culture Company Chairman Martin Bradley and Amanda Bradley, Pat McCafferty, Philip Gilliland (Londonderry Chamber) and Maoliosa Boyle (Void Gallery) with friends. © William Cherry, courtesy Culture Company.

I can think of no finer way to officially start the celebrations than a showcase of Derry's famous sons and daughters. The city's key assets have always been the place and its people. This concert represents the beginning of us showcasing our talents and creativity, and Ireland's entire north-west region on a global stage.

Culture Minister Carál Ní Chuilín

Above: Sons and Daughters concert line-up – including actors James Nesbitt, Eva Birthistle and Amanda Burton – pose for a photograph with Mayor Caoimhín Campbell and Deputy First Minister Martin McGuinness. Below left: Gary Lightbody and Derryman John McDaid of Snow Patrol pictured backstage at the concert. Below right: Mayor Caoimhín Campbell with Derry actresses Amanda Burton and Eva Birthistle at the Sons and Daughters concert. © William Cherry, courtesy Culture Company.

It makes you feel very proud that all these people are from Derry.

Dana

I am glad I am alive to see this.

Phil Coulter

Damian McGinty, Paul Brady and Neil Hannon performing at the Sons and Daughters concert. © William Cherry, courtesy Culture Company.

Irish music legends Paul Brady, Phil Coulter and Gary Lightbody with
Deputy First Minister Martin McGuinness backstage at the concert.
© William Cherry, courtesy Culture Company.

It's a chance to show what's great about the place.
Derry is a city that can really breathe now and
look forward with great excitement and pride.

Jimmy Nesbitt, host of Sons and Daughters

Nadine Coyle
backstage at the
Sons and Daughters
concert. © William
Cherry, courtesy
Culture Company.

Right: Actor Jimmy
Nesbitt with members of
the Codetta Choir.
© William Cherry,
courtesy Culture Company.

Above right: Deputy First Minister Martin McGuinness with daughters Grainne and Fionnuala at the Sons and Daughters concert.

Above left: Music producer Frank Gallagher with actress Eva Birthistle and musician Paul Brady, backstage at the concert.

Left: Derry music legends The Undertones with a young fan backstage.

Below left: Classical musical group The Priests, Fr Martin O'Hagan, Fr Eugene O'Hagan and Fr David Delargy.

Below: Mayor Caoimhín Campbell, Shona McCarthy, BBC NI Director Peter Johnston, Deputy First Minister Martin McGuinness and Corporate Sponsor Garvan O'Doherty. © William Cherry, courtesy Culture Company.

This girl's allowed to wow the crowd: Derry star Nadine Coyle. © William Cherry, courtesy Culture Company.

Snow Patrol in action. © William Cherry, courtesy Culture Company.

Just Say Yes: Gary Lightbody implores the millions watching the televised event to visit Derry during 2013.

Jump Boys: Derry music legends The Undertones get the crowd out of their seats. © William Cherry, courtesy Culture Company.

CONAL CRAICS THEM UP

Donegal comedian Conal Gallen entertains a full house at the
Millennium Forum. © Gavan Connolly.

February

Above and below: Young people from local schools welcome the news that the Radio One Big Weekend is to be staged in Derry. The announcement is made in the city live on the BBC by Radio One DJ Nick Grimshaw, who spends the day getting reaction from delighted would-be festival-goers. Included are: Mayor Caoimhín Campbell, Culture Company Chairman Martin Bradley and talented young singer-songwriter Bridie Monds-Watson (Soak). © Martin McKeown, courtesy Culture Company.

The month started with a bang, with the BBC decamping from London en masse to announce they would be staging one of Europe's top summer concerts – The Radio One Big Weekend – in Derry at the end of May. It would also be the first time ever the event would be held in the same city twice.

But the people of the Northwest didn't have to wait until summer to see some of the biggest names in music on their doorsteps. Philip King's Other Voices Festival, which specialises in bringing top acts to small venues, rolled into town on February 8, bringing names like Damien Dempsey, Beth Orton, Marina & The Diamonds and Derry's own Soak, Little Bear and Best Boy Grip onto our stages and (courtesy of RTÉ) our screens.

Other celebrations included a colourful pageant for the Chinese community to celebrate their New Year, while Nelson Drive – a former American naval camp turned housing development – marked its 50th birthday.

There was a major influx of visitors, too – thousands of scouts from all over Ireland braved the elements for a camping weekend at St Columb's Park, while the GAA hosted the finals of its annual Scór na nÓg talent show at The Venue.

We have an opportunity to build an enduring legacy over the next three years, share our knowledge and learning with the city and establish a renewable and refreshable resource, making this singing city audible and visible the world over.

Other Voices' organiser Philip King announces his event will return to Derry after its rapturous reception.

other voices

Bronagh Gallagher with Derry artist Paul Casey on bass. © Lorcan Doherty.

Bronagh Gallagher voicing her commitment to the city. © Lorcan Doherty.

James Yorkston. © Emmett McLaughlin.

The Other Voices Festival breathes new life into a former church on Great James Street. The newly styled Glassworks is now established as a prestigious location for cultural events. © Emmett McLaughlin.

California Dreamin': Top US singer Jesca Hoop drops in for a song. Courtesy Culture Company.

Simply Divine: Neil Hannon gives us something for the weekend. © Lorcan Doherty.

Soak-ed with talent: Bridie Monds-Watson. © Lorcan Doherty.

Best Boy Eoin O'Callaghan gives a gripping performance. Courtesy Culture Company.

Local musician and composer Katherine Philippa pauses for reflection. Courtesy Culture Company.

Shameless show-stealers, Little Bear. © Emmett McLaughlin.

A 24-carat performance from Marina & the Diamonds. © Lorcan Doherty.

Visiting Other Voices artist Marina Diamandis turns teacher for a day. Courtesy Culture Company.

Daughter vocalist Elena Tonra makes a new family of Derry fans. © Emmett McLaughlin.

Other Voices film an impromptu session featuring Bronagh Gallagher and Soak at Derry's independent record shop Cool Discs. Courtesy Culture Company.

Irish actor and presenter of Other Voices Aidan Gillen takes a tour of the city's famous walls with Bronagh Gallagher. Courtesy Culture Company.

Above left: Thousands of scouts from all over Ireland make their way across the Peace Bridge as the organisation celebrates Founder's Day, bringing to a conclusion a weekend of scouting activities which are centered at Ebrington Square in the city. Above right: Carndonagh scout Oisin Moyne ascends the climbing wall. Below: Amy O'Connell and Jade Jackson from St Eugene's Scouts in Derry set up camp near the Peace Bridge. © Martin McKeown, courtesy Culture Company.

Above left: A Chinese Dragon dance performance marks the Year of the Snake. Above right: Zhu Changhai and Richard Brown demonstrate the art of Tai Chi. Right: Je Lin performing a traditional fan dance at the City of Culture Chinese New Year celebrations in the Craft Village. © Martin McKeown/Inpresspics.com, courtesy Culture Company.

Young Sophia Byrne, aged 8, meets her favourite author, Australian Children's Laureate Alison Lester, at the Story Book Grow event at the Verbal Arts Centre. Courtesy Culture Company.

Above & opposite: Up to 2,000 people drawn from all over Ireland take part in the national finals of Scór na nÓg 2013 at The Venue. Scór is a GAA competition that combines all the colour and rivalry of Gaelic Games with the social/fun element of Ireland's traditional pastimes. Courtesy Culture Company.

In early spring, 'A' Level English students from schools across the Northwest assembled at special writing workshops where they received mentoring from Guildhall Press authors Dave Duggan, Felicity McCall and Freya McClements. Each pupil was then asked to write a short story based on a song or piece of music, and this culminated in a book entitled 'Soundtrack of our Lives', containing more than 50 stories, published in June. The initiative was convened by the St Columb's College Head of English and crime writer Brian McGilloway (above left) and supported by Culture Company, whose Chief Programmer Martin Melarkey attended the launch with his wife, Clare. Courtesy Culture Company.

Actor Howard Teale recreates the life of the legendary 18th-century Bishop of Derry Frederick Hervey in Ken McCormack's play 'On the Subject of Love' at the Playhouse. © Gavan Connolly.

44

Paul Casey, and Steven
McCool of Little Bear,
entertain a packed
Jammhouse at the Playhouse.
© Gavan Connolly.

These hands were made for walking: The Exchange Youth Project at the Playhouse. © Gavan Connolly.

Striking action: Kickboxing at the Tower Hotel. © Gavan Connolly.

In February, Echo Echo invite audiences to a lunchtime dance performance at their Bishop Street studios with music from the Henry Girls. © Simon Fallaha.

Caw/Nelson Drive 50th Anniversary Dinner

Members of Dolphin Dance School, Long Tower Dance School and McCloskey School of Dance performing at the Caw and Nelson Drive 50th Anniversary Dinner. © Lorcan Doherty.

Hold on to your teddy:
Children and parents enjoy a Dog
Ears' Humdinger Festival reading and
music event at the Central Library.
© John McDaid/Dog Ears.

As the days got longer and the weather a bit milder, so, too, the party began to heat up. Primal Scream, led by the eternally youthful Bobby Gillespie, hosted their only Northern gig of the year at The Venue. It was a complete triumph and widely reviewed as their best performance ever on these shores.

The new pavilion was also packed to the rafters in March for the London Symphony Orchestra, featuring Derry's own Mary Bergin on violin. The LSO were celebrating the film music of John Williams, which included the composer's scores from 'Jaws', 'Indiana Jones', 'Jurassic Park' and 'Superman'.

Derry's status as a world-leader in shirt design was celebrated, too, in the 'Off the Cuff' fashion competition, organised by students from Northern Ireland, Glasgow and Nuremburg.

And St Patrick's Weekend was marked with a spring carnival that included parades, concerts, open-air céilí-dancing and an Irish language day. Another saint celebrated in March was Colmcille, the city's patron saint, in the form of a new bronze statue erected in his honour in St Columb's Park.

The big international event of the month, however, was undoubtedly the Hofesh Shechter Dance Company's staging of 'Political Mother' at The Venue. Shechter – regarded as the world's greatest young choreographer – trained up local musicians to provide the soundtrack for his trademark piece. And he also recruited teams of talented young Derry dancers to perform an open-air preview show at the Craft Village.

The dance theme continued right through until the end of the month, when the Royal Ballet made their first appearance in the North in a decade. They performed selected highlights from their repertoire at The Venue, accompanied by an orchestra conducted by Derry-born Paul Murphy.

The city also set its first world record of the year when more than 5,400 Annies gathered at Ebrington Square to perform hits from the Broadway musical.

Get shirty: this Off the Cuff model sports a skirt made of shirt sleeves. © Martin McKeown, courtesy Culture Company.

Music and movies at The Venue. The London Symphony Orchestra celebrate the music of film-score legend John Williams, the genius behind the soundtracks to Indiana Jones (top) and Jurassic Park (below). © Martin McKeown, courtesy Culture Company.

51

Top left: Culture Company Executive Programmer Graeme Farrow with LSO Managing Director Kathryn McDowell. Above: An animated LSO conductor Frank Strobel. Left: LSO pulling strings in Derry. © Martin McKeown, courtesy Culture Company.

The Foyle Haven Arts Collective's production of 'Every Bottle has a Story to Tell' by Felicity McCall at the Playhouse. © Gavan Connolly.

Scenes from Dog Ears'
Humdinger Festival
of children's literature.
Included are celebrated
authors Julia Donaldson
('The Gruffalo'), Michael
De Souza ('Rastamouse')
and Roddy Doyle.
Courtesy Dog Ears.

*Loaded: A packed Venue welcomes
Primal Scream to Derry. © Martin
McKeown, courtesy Culture Company.*

Iconic Scottish rocker Bobby Gillespie gives a career-best performance for his Celtic cousins. The Primal Scream event is an early contender for gig of the year. © Martin McKeown, courtesy Culture Company.

Primal Scream in action. © Emmett McLaughlin.

Primal Scream applaud the audience. © Lorcan Doherty.

'Translations' playwright Brian Friel with Culture Company's Martin Melarkey.

Millennium Forum Productions presents

Translations

by

Brian Friel

directed by
Adrian Dunbar

The Millennium Forum played host to a large number of landmark events throughout the year. © Gavan Connolly.

A new production of Brian Friel's seminal play 'Translations', directed by Adrian Dunbar, opens at the Millennium Forum before embarking on a countrywide tour. Bottom left: President Michael D Higgins and his wife Sabina are special guests at the Dublin performance. Also included in photograph with cast members are David McLaughlin (Director, Millennium Forum) and Martin and Amanda Bradley. Courtesy Millennium Forum.

Off The Cuff

Models take to the catwalk for the Off the Cuff fashion competition at the North West Regional College. The term 'catwalk' is believed to have originated in Derry in the late 19th century when smartly dressed gentlefolk walking on Grand Parade on the city walls were subject to catcalls from local youths.
© Martin McKeown, courtesy Culture Company.

WHERE THERE IS PRESSURE THERE IS FOLKDANCE

HOFESH SHECHTER POLITICAL MOTHER

Hofesh Shechter, internationally renowned choreographer, brings his signature dance piece 'Political Mother' to The Venue for a two-night run. The Guardian salutes the 'deafening' performance as 'particularly special'. © Lorcan Doherty.

Scenes from 'Political Mother'. Courtesy Culture Company.

It felt like there was a scar…
this tension you can still feel.
I thought we really have to
blow some fresh air and hope,
and give young people a
sense of possibility.

Hofesh Shechter

Local dance groups take over the Craft Village with performances created by the Hofesh Shechter Company and inspired by 'Political Mother: Derry-Londonderry Uncut!' The young performers from the Dolphin Dance School and St Cecilia's College are joined by Mayor Caoimhín Campbell, Mark Ball, artistic director with LIFT, Shauna McNeilly, Culture Company, and Hofesh Shechter. Courtesy Culture Company.

And stretch: The Royal Ballet Company perform selected highlights from their repertory, conducted by Paul Murphy.
© Lorcan Doherty.

![THE MUSIC PROMISE]

*Above: Musician-in-Residence Neil Cowley and tutor
David Doherty pictured during a City of Culture 2013
Music Promise workshop at the Long Tower Youth Club.*

*Below: Composer Conor Mitchell pictured with members of
The Plantin' from Foyleview School as the school starts its
Music Promise journey. Included from left: Robert Canning,
Faustina O'Hagan, Dr Michael Dobbins, Principal, Sorcha
Friel, Denise White, music teacher, and Jason Welsh.
© Martin McKeown, courtesy Culture Company.*

*Left: A new nine-foot-tall statue of Derry's patron saint
Colmcille by Niall Bruton is unveiled in St Columb's Park.
The artist also produced twelve bronze-cast doves, which
form a Christian heritage trail from the Waterside to the city
centre. © Brendan McMenamin.*

The Playhouse hosts the ICAN (International Culture Arts Network) Project's two-day conference 'Challenging Place', examining how the arts challenge the people and place of Derry, drawing inspiration from national and international practitioners. © Gavan Connolly.

The Londonderry Musical Society (LMS) begin rehearsals for their production of Annie at The Venue. Courtesy Culture Company.

In the run-up to the LMS production of Annie, a new world record is set at Ebrington. Pictured here are the 5,500 people performing a song-and-dance routine from the show. Courtesy Culture Company.

Annie Harley from Culmore with her dog Sandy taking part in the world-record attempt. Courtesy Culture Company.

The sun will come out tomorrow! Above: Foyle MP Mark Durkan remains well wrapped up at Ebrington regardless. Courtesy Culture Company.

67

Annies of all ages at Ebrington. © Linda Heaney.

Aoibheann Biddle as Lily and David Keown as Rooster in the Londonderry Musical Society production of Annie. Courtesy Culture Company.

GAA Congress

This was the first time the GAA Congress, opened by President Michael D Higgins, was held outside Dublin. Hosted at The Venue, it was one of a series of major events brought by the GAA to the city during the year. Other events included the National Scór finals and Féile na nÓg.

Right: Joe Brolly gives the keynote speech at the National Congress. Above right: The commentator and former footballing All Star Jarlath Burns films Brolly's speech.
© Lorcan Doherty.

GAA ANNUAL CONGRESS DERRY 2013

Left: When Irish eyes are smiling. Megan O'Connor enjoying the parade.
Right: Mayor Caoimhín Campbell with Anne-Marie Gallagher and Dylan O'Doherty from the Fleadh committee, during Irish Language Day in Guildhall Square.
© Martin McKeown, courtesy Culture Company.

Scenes from the St Patrick's Day parade travelling through the city centre. © Martin McKeown, courtesy Culture Company.

St Patrick's Day event-support staff. © Linda Heaney.

St Patrick's Day parade. © Linda Heaney.

You have to take your hat off to the St Patrick's Day-parade. © Martin McKeown, courtesy Culture Company.

The Greater Shantallow Community Arts float. © Gavan Connolly.

Echo Echo stage the performance piece 'Without', a short distance outside the city walls. © Living Witness, courtesy Echo Echo.

Left: Teresa Campbell adds a splash of colour to her wedding dress for the Brides Across The Bridge record attempt.

Right: Tara O'Connor from Greysteel races to Guildhall Square. © Martin McKeown, courtesy Culture Company.

Yet another world record fell to Derry's irresistible charms in April, when more than 800 women re-donned their wedding gowns to take part in the 'Brides Across the Bridge' challenge. Quote of 2013 so far went to the husband who told the BBC he "broke out in a cold sweat" trying to get the zipper up on his wife's dress before she lined out on the Peace Bridge. And no, he didn't supply his name to the reporter.

Also crossing the Peace Bridge was the Dalai Lama, who returned to the city to visit his personal hero, Children in Crossfire director Richard Moore.

The second 'bridge', which sprang to prominence in April, was the card game. For the first time ever, the Irish Bridge Union hosted their Senior Congress and Senior Championships in the city.

The month also saw the world premiere of the feature film 'Jump', written by Derry woman Lisa Magee, and starring IFTA award-winner Ciaran McMenamin (right).

The city's status as the world's leading shirt-factory manufacturer was commemorated and celebrated in two plays – 'Factory Girls' by Frank McGuinness staged at the Forum, and Patsy Durnin's 'Tillies', which played to full houses at the Playhouse. Meanwhile, the artist Louise Walsh launched her own tribute to former workers in the form of a series of interviews and illustrations.

The London Street Gallery, curated by Noelle McAlinden, opened for business in April to exhibit work from both emerging and well-known local artists.

And London theatre company 11:18 – in conjunction with the Foyle Port – launched a new show 'The Farmer and the Fisherman' to run, not in a theatre, but in the Coleraine-Derry train. The play, which was set entirely amid the breathtaking Lough Foyle landscape, celebrated the connection between sea and rail transport in the Northwest.

The Brides Across the Bridge event is now set to be an annual event. © Martin McKeown, courtesy Culture Company.

I'm happy being single but always felt I'd missed out on the wedding day and all that comes with it, so when I heard about this I decided that I would have a proper reception for charity and invite all my pals. It's called Annie's Big Fat Bridal Party and we've had a ball!

Ann O'Neill
Derry hairdresser and first-time bride

Left: Artist Louise Walsh working with former machinists on her Shirt Factory Project. © Emmett McLaughlin.

Above: Director Vincent O'Callaghan with author Desmond Doherty and Paul Hippsley of Guildhall Press, filming the cinema-style trailer for the crime novel and enhanced eBook 'Valberg'. © Jim Hughes.

Below: Performers from the London theatre company 11:18 who staged their show 'The Farmer and the Fisherman' on the Coleraine-Derry train, pictured with, at back, Dolores O'Reilly from the Foyle Port. © Lorcan Doherty.

Opposite: Models taking part in the Bedlam Vintage Market and Catwalk Show, pictured here outside St Columb's Cathedral. © Gavan Connolly.

The Beyond the Walls exhibition at the City Factory. © Lorcan Doherty.

Artist Tom Agnew at the official opening of the Off the Cuff exhibition at the London Street Gallery. © Lorcan Doherty.

More Annie shenanigans. The LMS organise a flash mob at Foyle-side to promote the show. © Martin McKeown, courtesy Culture Company.

'Tillies' by Patrick Durnin is staged at the Playhouse to great acclaim. Included are performers Maureen Wilkinson, Kathy Deehan, Louise Conaghan, Rachel Melaugh and Maeve Connolly. © Gavan Connolly.

This must be the century of peace. My generation's century is now gone, but the future is still in your hands.

The Dalai Lama addresses Derry schoolchildren

THE DALAI LAMA IN DERRY

Many international statesmen and women visited the city during 2013 though few drew crowds like the Dalai Lama, who was invited as the special guest of Richard Moore to speak on the culture of compassion. The Tibetan spiritual leader regularly ignores protocol and his security detail to meet and greet the delighted Derry public. Featured in the photographs are: Richard Moore and Children in Crossfire staff, BBC journalist Michael O'Donnell, Portrait of a City trainer Terence Coyle, and members of the Moore family, including Pearse Moore Snr (shaking hands above), who sadly passed away in early 2014. © Lorcan Doherty.

Above: The official opening of the Irish Bridge Union's Midweek Senior Congress in the City Hotel. Included are: Ciara Burns, Chairperson NI Bridge Union, Mayor Caoimhín Campbell, Liam Hanratty, President CBAI, and Colm Duffy, sponsor, McCambridge Duffy and Company, Mary Kelly Rodgers, Pat McDevitt, Rex Anderson, Andrea Kelleher, Gareth Stewart and Mary McNamee, Culture Company, Jackie McAnee, Jim O'Sullivan, Harold Curran and John Bergin.

Left: At the gala premiere of the Derry feature film 'Jump' in the Brunswick Moviebowl are Kieron J Walsh, director, and Nichola Burley and Ciaran McMenamin, stars of the film. Courtesy Culture Company.

Portrait of a City launch

Pictured at the launch of the BT Portrait of a City digital archive project at the Glassworks: Landscape Ireland's Paul McGuckin and Andy Horsman, Mary Kay Mullan, Deirdre Nugent, Libraries NI, artist/photographer Jim Hughes (whose photograph was selected for the cover of the 2013 BT phone book), Michael McGuinness, Guildhall Press and artist Louise Walsh. Pictured below with Culture Company CEO Shona McCarthy and Mayor Caoimhín Campbell are representatives from the project sponsors: Peter Morris (BT), June Coates (Seagate) and Derry Credit Union President Philomena Deery. Courtesy Culture Company and © Phil Cunningham.

Let me entertain you. Surprise guest Robbie Williams hits the right note on the first day of the Radio One Big Weekend at Ebrington Square. © Tom Heaney.

A truly epic month swung into action with the four-day City of Derry Jazz & Big Band Festival, hosted at dozens of venues across the city, culminating in a gala Vintage Ball at Ebrington. Sticking with music, and the younger generation got a taste of things to come when Radio One DJ Nick Grimshaw hosted the BBC Music Academy at the Nerve Centre. The Script and Gabrielle Aplin made surprise appearances at the packed event.

But this was only the briefest of previews of what the BBC had in store for later in the month, when they would bring their Big Weekend to town. Every rumour was met – and bettered – as Bruno Mars, Ellie Goulding, Katy B, Robbie Williams, Biffy Clyro, and about 40 other world-class acts lined up in Derry for one of Europe's largest televised three-day festivals. The weekend wasn't without its drama either, with Calvin Harris and girlfriend Rita Ora forced to charter a private jet to Derry after gridlock seized Heathrow Airport.

Rita and Calvin were a week too late, however, to sample the ten-day festival organised to celebrate the most famous high-flier ever to visit the city – Amelia Earhart. The Earhart Festival – marking the 81st anniversary of the pilot's solo transatlantic flight – featured 40 different events and ended in a massive Vintage Ball.

Elsewhere, rehearsals got underway for the summer's biggest river-based event, the Return of Colmcille Festival. Indeed, the saint's legacy loomed large throughout these months, with more than 900 children and 40 teachers from primary schools taking part in the Digital Book of Kells project – where they created a series of animations inspired by the life and legacy of Colmcille. And there was lots of colour, too, from a team of 'craft-bombers', who set out to brighten up some of the city's less cultural spots – including the local police station!

Scenes from the Big Weekend. © Tom Heaney.

To have all the artists coming here is great. I would love this in Dublin.

Danny O'Donoghue, The Script frontman

DJs, musicians, actors and students at the BBC Radio One Academy at the Nerve Centre. Pictures include: Nick Grimshaw, Gabrielle Aplin, The Script's Danny O'Donoghue, Mark Sheehan and Glen Power, and EastEnders stars Nitin Ganatra, Jasymyn Banks and Tony Discipline. Participating students include Seanine Hasson, Sarah Higgins and Laura Dalton, who are taking part in a design workshop. © Martin McKeown, courtesy Culture Company.

Scenes from the Radio One Big Weekend. Photography © Tom Heaney.

Above: Chloe Donnelly, Bronagh Harkin and Caitlin Cooke. Below: Caroline Donnelly with Danny from The Script.

Labrinth (left) and Justin Young from The Vaccines (right) thrill the audience. © Tom Heaney.

Left: Caitlin Cooke, Aoife McCallion and Bronagh Harkin.
Below: Losing his shirt – a security man protects Dizzee from some
Derry rascals. © Tom Heaney.

Above: A jubilant audience at Ebrington. © Tom Heaney.

Scenes from the Radio One Big Weekend, courtesy Culture Company.

Some of the star-studded line-up gracing the stages at Ebrington, including: Iggy Azalea, Rita Ora, Calvin Harris and Olly Murs. Courtesy Culture Company.

The summer's biggest outdoor festival includes performances from The Saturdays, Katy B, Foals, Ellie Goulding, Biffy Clyro, Chase and Status, B.Traits and many more. Courtesy Culture Company.

Thanks for having me, Derry.

Robbie Williams

Above: Culture Minister Carál Ní Chuilín with daughter Cliodhna and Rosalie Flanagan enjoying the weekend.
© Tom Heaney.

> Radio One's Big Weekend was so impressive, it gave me goose-bumps listening to international music stars on the radio extolling the virtues of Derry, a place many of them probably had not heard of before.
>
> *Maggie Taggart*
> *BBC Arts Correspondent*

BBC RADIO 1'S BIG WEEKEND
DERRY~LONDONDERRY 2013

A large crowd gathers at the Gasyard Centre to watch the Radio One Big Weekend on the big screen.
© Bernard Ward.

*Radio One gives its final salute
to Derry in 2013 in the form of
a spectacular fireworks display on
the closing night. Producers say the
city provided the most picturesque
backdrop the event ever witnessed.
© Bernard Ward.*

Left: Three Choirs Choral, featuring Cantamus, Renaissance and Cathedral Choir at St Columb's Cathedral.
© Lorcan Doherty.

Left: The Chair of the Northern Ireland Tourism Board, Howard Hastings, visits the Apprentice Boys' Museum to announce a major funding package. Included on right is Apprentice Boys' General Secretary Billy Moore.
© Lorcan Doherty.

Opposite: Jenni Doherty gets her 'Writers Chair' signed by visiting author Melvyn Bragg at Little Acorns bookshop in Bedlam.

Above: Prince Michael of Kent (right) attends The Battle of the Atlantic 70th Anniversary Service and Commemoration at the Diamond War Memorial. Top right: Attending the commemorations are Police Commander Steven Martin, Stormont Speaker William Hay, April Garfield-Kidd, Drew Thompson, Gary Middleton and Maurice Devenney. © Lorcan Doherty.

Right: Culture Minister Carál Ní Chuilín lends a helping hand to the tug-o-war team from St Brigid's College, Derry, at the Celebrating Success in Sport showcase at The Venue. © Lorcan Doherty.

Bottom right: Karen Donnelly, granddaughter Chloe, Bernie McGowan and Marie Donnelly at the Foyle Hospice Female Fun run/walk at Ebrington.

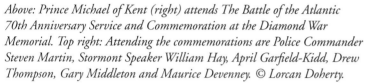

Above: Youngsters at the
Gordon Gallery enjoying
a selection of the winning
artwork from the Texaco
Annual Art Competition,
which had over 50,000
entries. © Deirdre Harte.

Musical feast at the Forum:
More than 1,500 school
children pack into the
Millennium Forum for a series
of Mayfest musical workshops.
© Lorcan Doherty.

Above: Punk music makes a welcome return in the form of Gary Mitchell's new drama 'Re-Energize' at the Playhouse. © Gavan Connolly.

Pupils from St Cecilia's College pose with cast and crew after an enjoyable performance of Ben Power's version of Shakespeare's 'Romeo and Juliet'. Directed by Bijan Sheibani and designed by Becs Andrews, it plays to packed Waterside Theatre audiences. © Roisin Clifford.

Young dancers are put through their paces at the Glassworks in preparation for the Return of Colmcille Pageant.
© Emmett McLaughlin.

Cradle of talent: Radio Foyle's Michael Bradley and Colmcille Pageant director Frank Cottrell Boyce examine some of the props for the June parade. Courtesy Culture Company.

Made In DERRY

Above: Comedian extraordinaire Noel McBride is in flying form here at the opening of the Earhart Festival. The much-loved funnyman sadly passed away in July 2013. © Gavan Connolly.

It's a marvel. The world's largest comic book (above), created by Joe Campbell, goes on display at Shantallow Library as part of the Earhart Festival. The graphic novel 'Distant Fields', which tells the story of four nationalist brothers who fought in World War I, is 42 feet long and almost six feet high. Pictured enjoying the artwork is author and playwright Felicity McCall. © Gavan Connolly.

Below: Slievemore pupils enjoy the Earhart parade. © Gavan Connolly.

Below: A capacity Guildhall Square crowd enjoys performances from Mickey Doherty and highlights from the musical Grease (above) as part of the Earhart Festival.
© Gavan Connolly.

Scenes from the Greater Shantallow Community Arts Earhart Festival include a community tea dance, a guest lecture by athlete and Everest climber Hannah Shields, and a colourful parade showcasing the area's young creative talent. © Gavan Connolly.

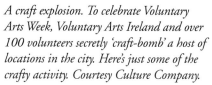

Craft Bomb

A craft explosion. To celebrate Voluntary Arts Week, Voluntary Arts Ireland and over 100 volunteers secretly 'craft-bomb' a host of locations in the city. Here's just some of the crafty activity. Courtesy Culture Company.

'Picturing Derry' launch. The Nerve Centre produces the first major photographic exhibition of the year at the City Factory. Curated by Declan Sheehan, it features pictures of the conflict taken by top local and international photographers. Included in the exhibition are images by the acclaimed Paris Match cameraman Gilles Caron which have never been displayed before.

Pictured at the launch are: (top left) Marjolaine Caron, Louis Bachelot, Gilles Caron Foundation, and Thierry Marlat, director of Marlat Gallery (Paris) and Declan Sheehan; (top centre) Eamon Melaugh; (top right) Willie Doherty; (above) John Peto, Martina Anderson MEP, Declan Sheehan and Pearse Moore; (middle right) Jim and Seosamh Collins; (left) Declan Sheehan, Pearse Moore, Vinny Cunningham, Martin Melarkey, John Peto, David Lewis and Graeme Farrow; (right) Willie Carson's daughters Oonagh & Mary, with grandchildren Ronan Hagan, Tess, Jude and Lana McConnell. Courtesy Culture Company.

Above: The JayDee Brass Band from the Netherlands making its way down Shipquay Street during the city's Jazz and Big Band Festival.

Top right: Jiving in Guildhall Square and Waterloo Place during the Jazz Festival. © Gavan Connolly.

Below: Local musicians taking part in a jazz workshop in the Verbal Arts Centre with the JayDee Brass Band. © Lorcan Doherty.

Peter Mc Kane

Jazz at the Playtraíl

Scenes from Jazz Festival events held at the Playtrail. Courtesy Peter McKane.

Grainne, Eimear and Ryan McAllister enjoying the fun at the Playtrail.

Above: Jazz Festival street parade on Shipquay Street. © Gavan Connolly. Right: The GI Girls, Emma McCrory, Marie Browne, Tracey McErlean and Carmel McGeady. Top right: Leeanne Doherty and Philip Wallace pictured at the Grand Vintage Ball featuring The Puppini Sisters at The Venue. Courtesy Culture Company.

Jenni Doherty and Kitty Jakeman at the Vintage Ball.

Peter and Erin Hutcheon.

Shauna McNeilly and Claire McDermott.

Gareth Doherty – jazz clown!

Mary Blake and Noelle McAlinden.

Ronan McCullough Trio at the Central Bar.

Michaela McGillion.

Second Line Jazz Parade.

Above and below: Andrew Monk performing in the Millennium Forum during the Jazz Festival. Courtesy Andrew Monk.

Me and my shadow. It's wall-to-wall jazz across the city. © Vinny Cunningham.

Jiving in Henderson Music during the Jazz Festival. © Gavan Connolly.

On yer bike. Hundreds of people – young and old – take part in the first-ever Wild Walls Cycle. Courtesy Culture Company.

Nicola Rodgers at the Vintage Ball. Courtesy Culture Company.

Marcella Puppini bewitches the crowd at The Venue and Paul McIntyre entertains at the Playhouse. Courtesy Culture Company.

June

June sees the colourful Sky Orchestra bring music from the heavens. Hot-air balloons carrying giant speakers ascend over the Foyle Bridge on Midsummer morning. © Emmett McLaughlin.

The LegenDerry Nessie. © Brendan McMenamin.

As June arrived, the volume was cranked up to 11 – and it would stay cranked up for the rest of the summer.

There was a non-stop cavalcade of events – the undoubted centrepiece of which was the Return of Colmcille Festival, staged right across the city and along the River Foyle. The June 9 pageant, directed by Frank Cottrell Boyce, portrayed the 21st-century homecoming of the city's exiled patron saint. A cast of thousands – watched by tens of thousands – took part in the huge and colourful showcase, which celebrated Derry's proud history since Colmcille's tearful departure at the end of the 6th century.

Midsummer saw the city thronged again as thousands of musicians took part in Derry's first-ever Music City event – a dawn-to-dusk extravaganza of local talent, playing everywhere from street corners to Ebrington Square. The June 21 musical marathon got underway with the Dawn Chorus at Grianan of Aileach, the ancient Celtic sun-palace just outside the city. And for those who couldn't make it, the Sky Orchestra – comprising seven hot-air balloons, all with music blasting from speakers – flew over the city at sun-up to kickstart the special event. Yet another world record was set on Guildhall Square at lunchtime,

choral rendition of the city's best-known anthem, 'Danny Boy'. Many hours, and many songs, later, the day concluded with a joyous and riotous, certainly not-unplugged, gig at Ebrington, which kept the entire city awake into the wee hours.

The following night, more than 4,000 rock fans were back on their feet for the hirsute highlight of the year – Status Quo at The Venue. And the music wasn't finished yet. Elvis Costello hosted a stormer of a gig a few nights later at the same venue. And as the month drew to a close, the Celtronic Festival attracted massive crowds from all over Ireland and beyond.

For those whose eardrums couldn't take any more, there were some slightly more contemplative cultural offerings to be had, in the form of Rita Duffy's much-acclaimed Shirt Factory installation on Patrick Street and The Big Weave at St Augustine's Church.

On the sporting front, there was the first Walled City Marathon in 25 years and also a huge river-based triathlon. But there was no escaping the beat entirely – even at events such as the Ubuntu World Food Festival, where diners were accompanied by some of the finest World music ever heard in the city. Few, if

Acrobats and street dancers in action at the Return of Colmcille Festival. © Gavan Connolly (left). © John Boyle (right).

Left: A character from the Return of Colmcille Pageant. © Martin McKeown, courtesy Culture Company.

The city centre is turned upside down for the day, as the streets fill with onlookers and performers. Included (right) are: Writer Anita Robinson and lawyer Gregory McCartney © Martin McKeown, courtesy Culture Company.

The punk-music scene in the city is well represented with The Undertones taking centre stage on the day and a procession around the Guildhall led by scooter enthusiasts John O'Hara and Ciaran McCorry. © Gavan Connolly.

Punk Subbuteo, a tribute to The Undertones' song 'My Perfect Cousin'. © Gavan Connolly.

Left: Punk paraders. © Martin McKeown, courtesy Culture Company.

Undertones singer Paul McLoone ushers in the summer with the help of thousands of Derry natives. © Martin McKeown, courtesy Culture Company.

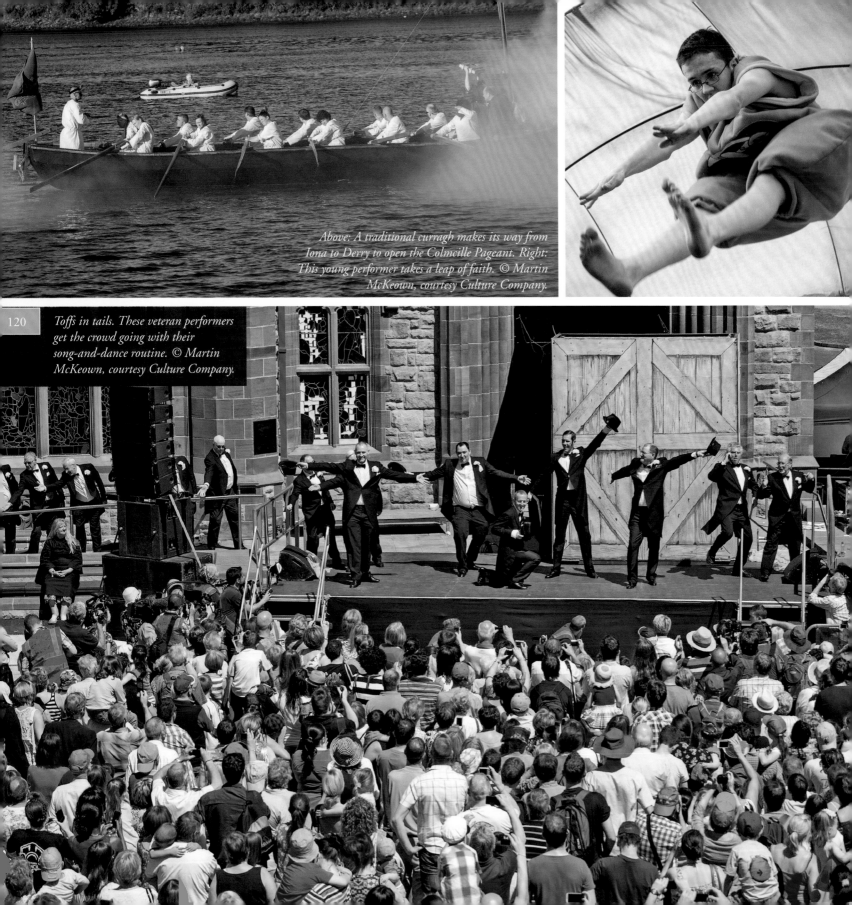

Above: A traditional curragh makes its way from Iona to Derry to open the Colmcille Pageant. Right: This young performer takes a leap of faith. © Martin McKeown, courtesy Culture Company.

Toffs in tails. These veteran performers get the crowd going with their song-and-dance routine. © Martin McKeown, courtesy Culture Company.

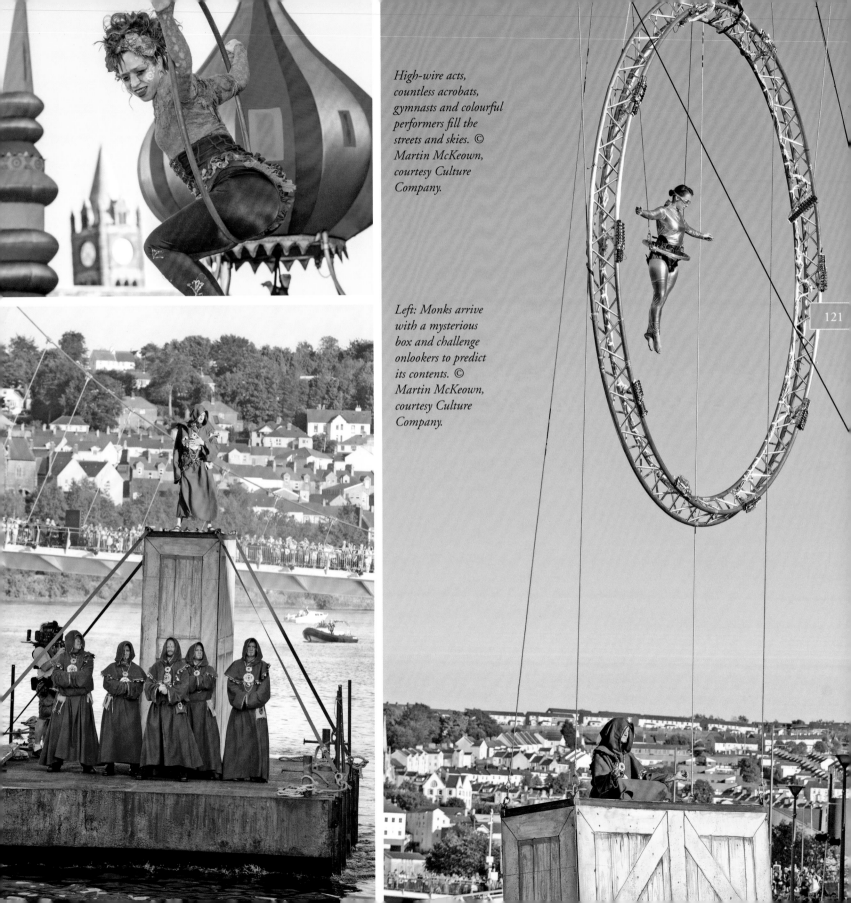

High-wire acts, countless acrobats, gymnasts and colourful performers fill the streets and skies. © Martin McKeown, courtesy Culture Company.

Left: Monks arrive with a mysterious box and challenge onlookers to predict its contents. © Martin McKeown, courtesy Culture Company.

Dopey Dick, the lost killer whale who last surfaced in Derry in 1977, makes a welcome reappearance. © Martin McKeown, courtesy Culture Company.

Dignitaries backstage at the Guildhall: Justice Minister David Ford, Martina Anderson MEP, Martin Bradley, Culture Company, Mayor Martin Reilly, Culture Minister Carál Ní Chuilín, Deputy First Minister Martin McGuinness and Shona McCarthy, Culture Company. © Martin McKeown, courtesy Culture Company.

Shirt-factory girls thread their way through the streets.

High-wire antics at the Return of Colmcille. © Bertie Whiteside.

Colourful scenes from the Return of Colmcille Pageant. More than 30,000 people swarm into the city centre for the largest community event of the year. © Martin McKeown, courtesy Culture Company.

© Carol Cunningham.

No fear of heights here! A low-flying Amelia Earhart joins in the fun. © Martin McKeown, courtesy Culture Company.

NR-7952

Fashion and dance at London Street. © Martin McKeown, courtesy Culture Company.

The contents of the mysterious box reveal the story of Derry as told by its children. © Martin McKeown, courtesy Culture Company.

Colour and culture on the city-centre streets. © Phil Cunningham.

All aboard: the Oceans' Parade at Ebrington. Below: Remembering the war years – jivers and GIs. © Gavan Connolly.

Opposite: Let's dance. © John Boyle.

The Nerve Centre hosts a colourful celebration to launch the Digital Book of Kells, which involved over 900 schoolchildren from the city creating animations inspired by the life and legacy of Colmcille. © Martin McKeown, courtesy Culture Company.

Below: A sun-baked Guildhall Square welcomes thousands to the big party. © Brendan McMenamin.

Above: Politicians Mark Durkan, Martin McGuinness and Martin Reilly make their way across Union Hall Place to the Guildhall for the Columban celebrations. © Phil Cunningham.

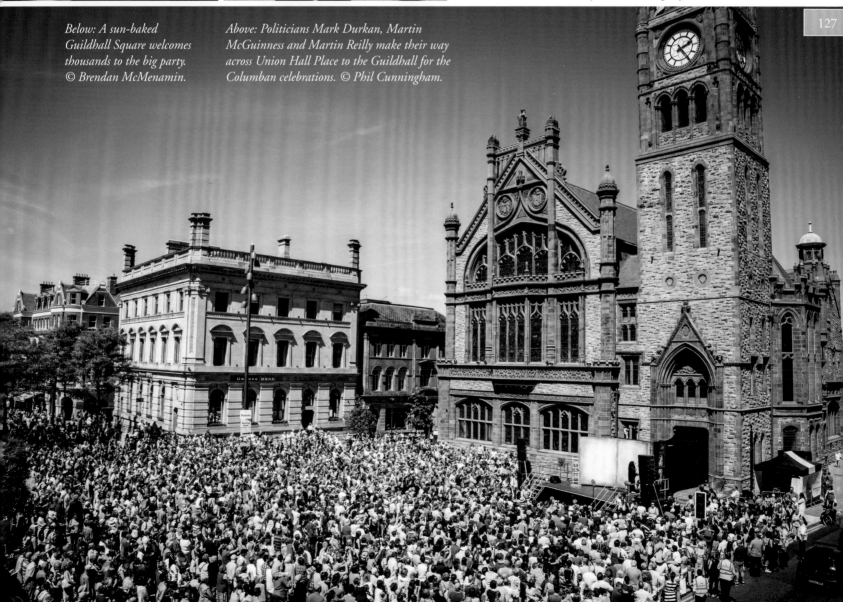

128

The city's senses are bombarded with a myriad of sights, smells and sounds. © Emmett McLaughlin.

Clowning around at the Return of Colmcille. © Martin McKeown, courtesy Culture Company.

Up, up and away: a mystic monk is carried aloft a giant incense vessel. © John Boyle.

Colour and grace everywhere at the Return of Colmcille. © Emmett McLaughlin.

The new book of Colmcille opens a door to the city's cultural future. © Emmett McLaughlin.

The Foyle heats up for the grand finale. © Emmett McLaughlin.

No smoke without fire:
acrobats and performers
set the city ablaze.
© Emmett McLaughlin.

© Gavan Connolly.

© Brendan McMenamin.

© Pam Hardeman.

132

Saint Colmcille is the first person to have seen the Loch Ness monster, and he's coming back for a massive showdown on the Foyle on Saturday night!

Frank Cottrell Boyce, setting the stage for an epic river battle.

© *Brendan McMenamin.*

134

Images © Bernard Ward.

Images © Martin McKeown, courtesy Culture Company.

Crowds pack the banks of the Foyle to witness the finale, as seen from the roof of the City Hotel. © Emmett McLaughlin.

© Emmett McLaughlin.

Nessie no more. The celebrations end in a giant pyrotechnic battle which sees Colmcille emerge victorious.
© Martin McKeown.

The Dawn Chorus

Scenes from Grianan, County Donegal, captured by photographers Emmett McLaughlin and Stephen Boyle. Hundreds of singers gather at daybreak to sing in the arrival of Midsummer Day. The morning festivities are led by the Inishowen Gateway Choir and continue throughout the day with performances and displays of processional sculpture, aerial acrobatics, dancing fire, illuminated installation, sumptuous costume and music written by Liam Ó Maonlaí of Hothouse Flowers.

Jilly St John from the band Wyldling at Grianan, overlooking some of the finest views in Ireland.
© Emmett McLaughlin

Local fiddle players Denise Wilkinson and Merle Drost at the Dawn Chorus.

Six miles from Grianan, just outside Derry, the Sky Orchestra prepares for its own dawn spectacle. A host of hot-air balloons – all piping out classical music – drift across the skies of the Northwest.

www.balloonflights.ie

Below: Fearless Culture Company staff Grainne Devine, Emmett McLaughlin and Shona McCarthy get ready for lift-off.

144

@ Brendan McMenamin

Mayor Martin Reilly tweets a quick pic of what's ahead of him. © Stephen Boyle.

Intrepid photographer Emmett McLaughlin captures these unique images with only a thin wicker basket floor between him and the lush green fields of Donegal.

Above: The Sky Orchestra soars over the city. © Gavan Connolly.

Below: Emmett McLaughlin captures a bird's-eye view of the city.

In sunshine and in shadow. Thousands throng Guildhall Square to set the world record for the greatest number of choristers gathered at the one site to sing the Derry anthem 'Danny Boy'.
© Gavan Connolly.

150

Sounds of the city: June 21 sees an explosion of music across the entire cityscape to mark the inaugural Music City day. Above: Wonder Villains at Ebrington Square. Below: The Buena Vista Social Club at The Venue. © Gavan Connolly.

Above: Paddy Nash & the Happy Enchiladas headline Music City at Ebrington Square while (below) Status Quo have them rocking in the aisles at The Venue the following night.
© Gavan Connolly.

BBC correspondent Mark Simpson gets into the swing of Music City. © Damien McClelland.

Little Bear join the party.

© Damien McClelland.

© Emmett McLaughlin.

Quo give the crowd whatever they want. © Gavan Connolly.

Music City at the Gasyard. © Gavan Connolly.

The Pink Ladies at the Gasyard. © Gavan Connolly.

Conal McFeely with The Morgan O'Kane Band at Ráth Mór on Music City day.

Young singers from St John's PS rocking out with Paddy Nash and Diane Greer at Ráth Mór on Music City day. © Nathaniel Harkin.

Songstress Bronagh Gallagher visits Guildhall Press as part of a BBC programme she is researching on music in Derry. She is welcomed by Michael McGuinness, Patsy Durnin and Paul Hippsley.

Musician-in-Residence Neil Cowley on Music City day at St Augustine's. © Gavan Connolly.

The whole city is a stage for Music City day. © Gavan Connolly.

The 2013 Celtronic Festival, directed by Gareth Stewart, is the biggest electronic music/dance event of the year. Numerous workshops and gigs take place throughout the city featuring top acts such as Chic, Ewan Pearson, Metro Area, Tom Middleton, Jon Hopkins, Bicep, David Kitt, Move D, John Talbot, Nina Kraviz, DJ Hell, Henrik Schwarz and a host of other big names.

Above & below: Pupils from Rosemount PS performing for shoppers in Foyleside on Music City day. © Damien Stewart.

Public Service Broadcasting.

A Tom Middleton workshop at the Glassworks facilitated by Blast Furnace studios.

celtronic 2013

celtronic

Crowd enjoying Jon Hopkins at the Nerve Centre. © Emmett McLaughlin.

155

Kids' Disco at the Gasyard.

Henrik Schwarz at the Gweedore.

*All aglow at the
Celtronic Kids' Disco.*

Tom Middleton.

*Scenes from Celtronic 2013.
© Emmett McLaughlin.*

Nina Kraviz.

DJ Hell.

Pariah.

DJ Hell at St Columb's Hall.

Above: Celtronic photographer Emmett McLaughlin and Lindsay Ellis from Yorkshire enjoying the craic. Below: Gareth Stewart and Caolan Harkin, Celtronic.

Francesco Tristano.

158

Celtronic showcases innovative events across the city in spaces such as the Glassworks. © Emmett McLaughlin.

Ewan Pearson at the Glassworks.

A colourful Celtronic event at St Columb's Hall.

Hago at the Craft Village

Celtronic events at the Craft Village.

Filmmaker Ronan Carr and musician/ artist James Cunningham.

Children's art festival at the Playhouse. © Áine McCarron.

As part of the Purposeful Inquiry strand of 2013, the Pat Finucane Centre host an international human rights conference, 'Poisonous Legacies', at the Guildhall with speakers from the Balkans, Spain, the Basque Country, South Africa, Palestine and Israel. Included are: Andree Murphy (Relatives for Justice), Mary McCallum (Wave), Bill Rolston (Transitional Justice Institute), and Seamas Heaney (Healthy Living Centre).

A scene from 'The Cook' at the Playhouse. The drama by Georgia Rhoades tells the tragic story of an 18th-century Derry bishop's servant who was executed by burning at the stake for child murder. © Gavan Connolly.

Guildhall Press author Desmond Doherty (right) at the launch of his debut novel 'Valberg' at the City Hotel with guest Charlie McGuigan. © Stephen Boyle.

The Big Weave at St Augustine's Church celebrates aspects of the city's heritage in the form of textiles. © Deirdre Harte.

Above: Apple co-founder Steve Wozniak and Eden Project founder Sir Tim Smit speaking to Noribic chief Dr Barney Toal before the European Business Network's annual conference, being held in Ireland for the first time. Pictured below at the EBN conference are Derry guests Peter Gallagher, Joanna McConway, John Hume and Aine Gallagher. © Lorcan Doherty.

The first Walled City Marathon in almost three decades gets underway. Images © Tom Heaney.

YOU ARE NOW ENTERING THE FINAL STAGE OF THE WALLED CITY MARATHON 2013

Veteran athlete Tommy Hughes breaks the tape to win the marathon more than 25 years after he last won the same event.

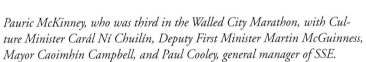

Pauric McKinney, who was third in the Walled City Marathon, with Culture Minister Carál Ní Chuilín, Deputy First Minister Martin McGuinness, Mayor Caoimhín Campbell, and Paul Cooley, general manager of SSE.

The inaugural City of Culture Triathlon is won by Olympic athletes Gavin Noble and Aileen Reid (Derry).

Triathlon organiser Peter Jack interviews women's winner Aileen Reid at the finish line. Photography © Phil Cunningham.

Artist Rita Duffy at the launch of her Shirt Factory Project at the City Factory. © Emmett McLaughlin.

Fashion designer Joe Carlin with Grainne Devine (right) and friend.

This year-long project has worked with various individuals, stitching together a range of themes; history, politics, gender roles, collective lived experience, economics etc, presenting what we came up with in various ways in the environment of a pop-up museum.

Rita Duffy, Director of the Shirt Factory Project

Carita Kerr, centre, with Cara Mooney, right, and guest.

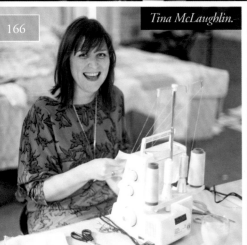

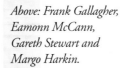

Tina McLaughlin.

Above: Frank Gallagher, Eamonn McCann, Gareth Stewart and Margo Harkin.

Right: Cara Mooney performing a song in tribute to the factory girls. Below right: Mairéad Carlin sings 'Scarlet Ribbons', a factory favourite.

Marty Doherty and daughter Christina Louise.

2D NORTHERN IRELAND COMICS FESTIVAL

Above: 2D Festival founder, and graphic artist, David Campbell is captured by the Emerald Garrison Troupe in the Millennium Forum. Courtesy David Campbell.

The hugely successful 2D Festival celebrates the work of graphic artists, provides educational opportunities for aspiring artists, and showcases national and international comic-industry professionals (including local artists Uproar Comics pictured below). It attracts record attendances in 2013.

168

A taste of the Ubuntu World Food Festival at St Columb's Park. Entertainment includes performances from In Your Space, Granny Tourismo, cooking demonstrations from Emmett McCourt, storytelling, art workshops and live music. © Emmett McLaughlin.

The city's vibrant multicultural identity is showcased here and opposite in song, dance, cuisine and craic with children and adults enjoying the many cultural performances and activities laid on as part of the Ubuntu World Food Festival. © Emmett McLaughlin.

A piper prepares to greet the huge gathering of soccer fans packing Guildhall Square for the opening ceremony of the 2013 Foyle Cup. © Lorcan Doherty.

July

By the height of the summer, tens of thousands of new tourists were pouring into the city from all over the world. And there was something for all tastes.

The biggest hit – not to mention the *Derry Journal*'s gig of 2013 – was Chic, fronted by New York club god Niles Rodgers. Their Disco Inferno at The Venue proved so popular, they immediately signed up for a return visit at Halloween.

The 400th anniversary of the city walls was commemorated in a new cantata written by poet Paul Muldoon and composer Marc Anthony Turnage. 'At Sixes and Sevens' was premiered simultaneously at the London and Derry Guildhalls. There were further treats for classical fans, too, in the form of appearances by Cathal Breslin and Katia Labeque, among others, at the ten-day Walled City Music Festival.

The island's pipers assembled at St Columb's Park in July, too, for the 68th All-Ireland Pipe Band Championships. Meanwhile, performers from August's Walled City Tattoo travelled to Westminster to give Londoners a taste of what to expect the following month.

While the city's Elizabethan ramparts were marking their 400th birthday, other less celebrated walls were getting a makeover, courtesy of the world's best graffiti artists, who landed in town for a spray-can showdown.

There was sport aplenty, too, with more than 200 youth football teams from all over the world parading into town for the Foyle Cup. Prehen hosted a Pro-Am golf tournament, Bready organised a one-day cricket international, and The Venue staged international judo and wrestling competitions.

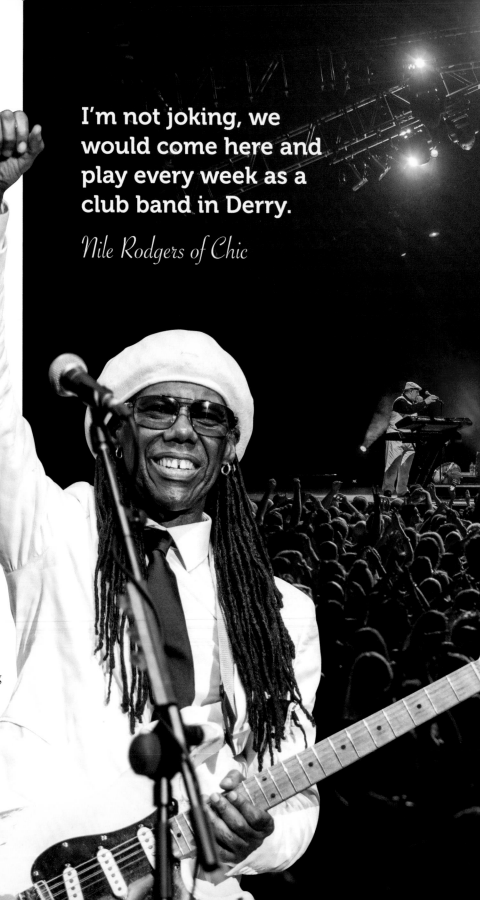

I'm not joking, we would come here and play every week as a club band in Derry.

Nile Rodgers of Chic

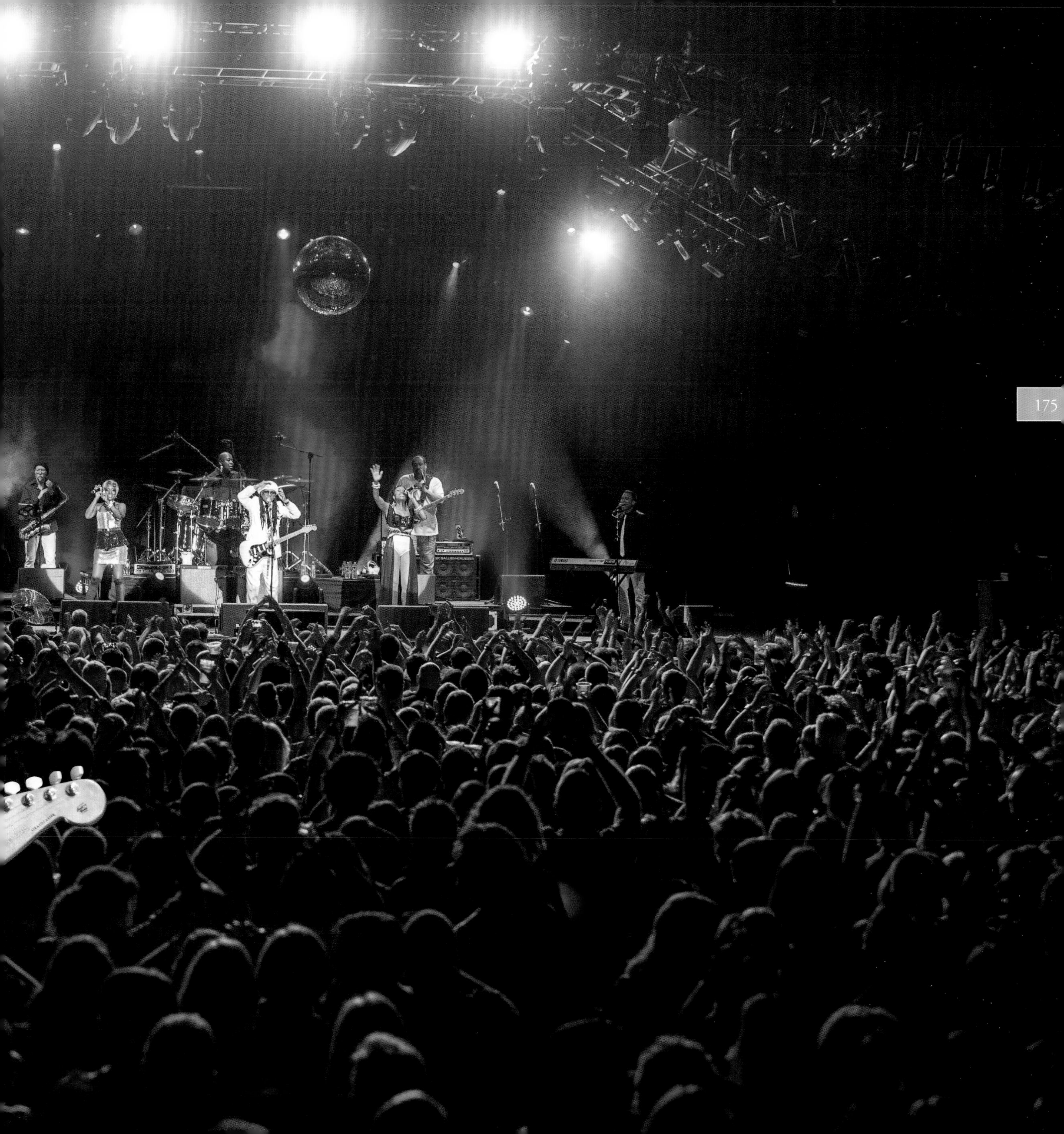

Everybody dance: Chic's sell-out concert in July is so successful they are immediately rebooked to headline the Halloween celebrations. © Emmett McLaughlin.

178

Chic welcome Culture Company staff, family and friends on stage to end the show. Included in these images are: Claire McDermott, Siobhán O'Reilly, Mark Nagurski, Brian Fisher, Larry Deeney and Shona McCarthy.

Left: CultureTech Director Mark Nagurski takes a few snaps of the show from the stage. His shot above captures the large audience.

Award-winning German photographer Kai Wiedenhoffer gives Free Derry Corner a makeover with his 'Wall on Wall' image to launch the Beyond The Walls project in July. The same image is erected simultaneously on the Berlin Wall to bring the two landmarks together through art. © Lorcan Doherty.

Snow Patrol star John McDaid, the first Pushkin Prize winner, with the Duchess of Abercorn and Helen Cannon, Editor, Pushkin Trust Voices – a collection of memories and experiences celebrating the first 25 years of the Pushkin Trust, launched at the Verbal Arts Centre. © Lorcan Doherty.

Above: Some of the world's leading street/graffiti artists from USA, Germany, Ireland and Britain gather in the city to join with the best local artists for a two-day Graffiti Jam organised by Donal O'Doherty, Switch Skatepark.

Bottom left & below: Rehearsals for 'At Sixes and Sevens', a new cantata commissioned from Northern Irish poet Paul Muldoon and composer Mark Anthony Turnage. The world premiere is later performed simultaneously in the Guildhalls of London and Derry by Camerata Ireland and conductor Barry Douglas. Included in the image is the photojournalist and filmmaker Mark McCauley. Courtesy Culture Company.

As part of the Music Promise project, more than 200 young singers, dancers and musicians stage a massive new theatre piece 'Lenanshee' at The Venue.
Below: Director Connor Mitchell is pictured during rehearsals with members of the cast. Back left is singer Annie Doherty. © Martin McKeown,
courtesy Culture Company.

The year couldn't go by without the return of the city's most famous film and TV star, Hollywood legend Roma Downey. The actress – who had just finished her epic mini-series The Bible – is pictured here during a visit to the Guildhall with Culture Company Chairman Martin Bradley. Courtesy Culture Company.

Above: Everton midfielder Darron Gibson returns to his native Derry to launch the Hughes Insurance Foyle Cup 2013. Included with Darron on the city's historic walls are local Derry and District Youth players Adam Carr, Ciaran McLaughlin, David Arthur and Caoimhin O'Neill. © Lorcan Doherty.

Left: Paul Noonan (Bell X1) signs a hand-crafted board marking the release of their latest CD at Cool Discs record store. Courtesy Lee Mason.

Below: Action from the International Judo and Wrestling Championship at The Venue in Ebrington. Courtesy Culture Company.

Above: The 68th All-Ireland Pipe Band Championship at St Columb's Park. Sixty-one bands take part in the event hosted by the Royal Scottish Pipe Band Association NI Branch and the Irish Pipe Band Association. Deputy Mayor Gary Middleton is included as host.

East Londonderry MP Gregory Campbell welcomes performers from the Walled City Tattoo, including dancers Georgina Kee and Arlene McLaughlin (left), to the Houses of Parliament to give Londoners a taste of what to expect from the August event. Courtesy Culture Company.

Ebrington Square
Derry-Londonderry
Wed 28 - Fri 30 Aug 2013

Scenes from the Walled City Music Festival. Included are: Matthew Greenall, Paul Moore, Cathal Breslin, Sabrina Hu, Jeffrey Zeigler, Marie Louise Muir, and Kirill Troussov. Courtesy Walled City Music Festival.

Wile craic: Family and friends of the late Seamus McConnell launch the City of Culture edition of the 'Wile Big Derry Phrasebook', published by Guildhall Press, at the Central Library.

Yer head's a marley, mucker. Having fun at the 'Wile Big Derry Phrasebook' launch.

Another world record bites the dust as thousands of dancers, led by TV celebrity Eamonn Holmes, perform a mass Riverdance at Ebrington in aid of Children in Crossfire. © Lorcan Doherty.

it be LegenDerry

August

Just when you thought 2013 couldn't get any more massive, August struck. An estimated 430,000 Irish traditional music enthusiasts (i.e. four times the population of Derry) congregated in the city for Fleadh Cheoil na hÉireann. It was the first time the ten-day event had been held in the North and it proved massively popular with all sections of the community, with Ulster Scots musicians and artists playing a full part in the events. Yet another record was smashed, too, when 2,500 jiggers and reelers lined the Peace Bridge and Ebrington Square for the world's biggest ever Riverdance.

There was barely time to draw breath after the Fleadh left town before the Walled City Tattoo got underway at Ebrington – again attracting capacity, cross-community crowds. The 4,000-seater outdoor event included celebrations of the city's naval and shirt-factory heritage, all performed in a blazing mass of colour.

Colour was the name of the day also when Foyle Pride marked its 20th anniversary with a huge celebration in the city centre. Both Free Derry Corner and the Guildhall clock were turned pink for the occasion!

The month ended with Billy Bragg headlining the three-day Music for a New Revolution at the Nerve Centre. The event, which was organised by Derry's own Paddy Nash, celebrated and showcased the work of a host of top political/social songwriters.

On a sadder note, Seamus Heaney made his last-ever public appearance as part of the Fleadh, performing with the master piper Liam Óg O'Flynn in The Poet and The Piper. Heaney alluded to his tiredness as he left the Forum stage at the end of the night, but it was a terrible shock – and sense of loss – to the city when our Nobel son passed away just a fortnight later on August 30.

Shipquay Street is a sea of music lovers, gathered from all over the world for the All-Ireland Fleadh.
© Gavan Connolly.

189

Above: A view from the stage of the huge crowd gathered at Guildhall Square for the opening of the Fleadh. © Lorcan Doherty.

Left: Ethan Deery from St Anne's PS busking during the Fleadh.

Right: Terence Donnelly and his mother Mae enjoying the Fleadh at Ebrington.

Bottom left: Gearóid Ó hEára, Fleadh organiser, with Eibhlín Ní Dhochartaigh, Phil Coulter, Mayoress Bronagh Reilly and Mayor Martin Reilly at the opening of the Fleadh. © Lorcan Doherty.

Bottom middle: Derry author Phil Cunningham with the Manchester Rose during a visit by the international roses to the city during the Fleadh.

Bottom right: Briege Donnelly, Mae Donnelly and Cathy Falconer.

Opposite: Scenes from the opening-night spectacular of the Fleadh. Included are President Michael D Higgins, Mary Dillon and friends, Cara Dillon, and Francie and Anne Brolly. © Lorcan Doherty.

192

A colourful night of stars at the Craft Village. © Anna Czajak.

Bronagh Gallagher and Paul Casey are accompanied by TG4 presenter Gino Lupari in a trad seisiún at the Fleadh. © Emmett McLaughlin.

The Fleadh is a hotbed of young entrepreneurs. © Phil Cunningham.

Above: Young musicians perform in the shadow of the city walls. Left: A shop window to Irish culture. Two young dancers perform a reel in Austins Department Store. © Gavan Connolly

Trad with attitude! © Anna Czajak.

This was the biggest Fleadh ever. It was the biggest by fifty percent.

Labhrás Ó Múrchu
Director General of Comhaltas
Ceoltóirí Éireann

Music lovers of all ages join in the fun.
© Bernard Ward.

Look, Mammy, no seat!
© Phil Cunningham.

A seisiún breaks out in one of the many pop-up Fleadh bars.
© Bernard Ward.

Future Irish music legends at Magazine Gate. © Phil Cunningham.

Put your hands up if you love trad music.
© Bernard Ward.

Above: Two performers and their miniature orchestra.
© Dan Cullen. Below: Film crews capture an
impromptu session. © Michael Harkin.

Classical legend Gerard McChrystal (right)
tries his hand at trad. © Dan Cullen.

Last Visit of a Legend

Derry photographer Lorcan Doherty captured these memorable pictures of Seamus Heaney's last-ever public performance, which was held at the Millennium Forum. The Nobel Laureate was hosting an evening of poetry and music accompanied by the piper Liam Óg O'Flynn. Just over a fortnight later, only hours after the poet's death was announced, the musician Billy Bragg paid him a memorable tribute on stage at the Nerve Centre in Derry, reading the uplifting Heaney tract from 'The Cure at Troy', which was widely accepted as the inspiration for the 2013 cultural year. The day after the poet's death, hordes of people queued to sign a book of condolence at the Guildhall.

The presence of Seamus was a warm one, full of humour, care and courtesy — a courtesy that enabled him to carry, with such wry Northern Irish dignity, so many well-deserved honours from all over the world.

President Michael D Higgins pays tribute to Derry's Poet Laureate.

Above: Billy Bragg reads from 'The Cure of Troy' at the Nerve Centre.

Right: Renowned Irish piper Liam Óg O'Flynn with Seamus Heaney at the Forum.

Below: A tribute from Deputy First Minister Martin McGuinness in the book of condolence at the Guildhall. © Lorcan Doherty.

31.8.13   Martin McGuinness   Derry City   For Seamus,
the humble Bellaghy man
who became Ireland's National
Treasure.
Running water never disappointed
Crossing water always furthered
something
Stepping stones were stations
of the soul.
Le grá Togetherness Abú.
Martin

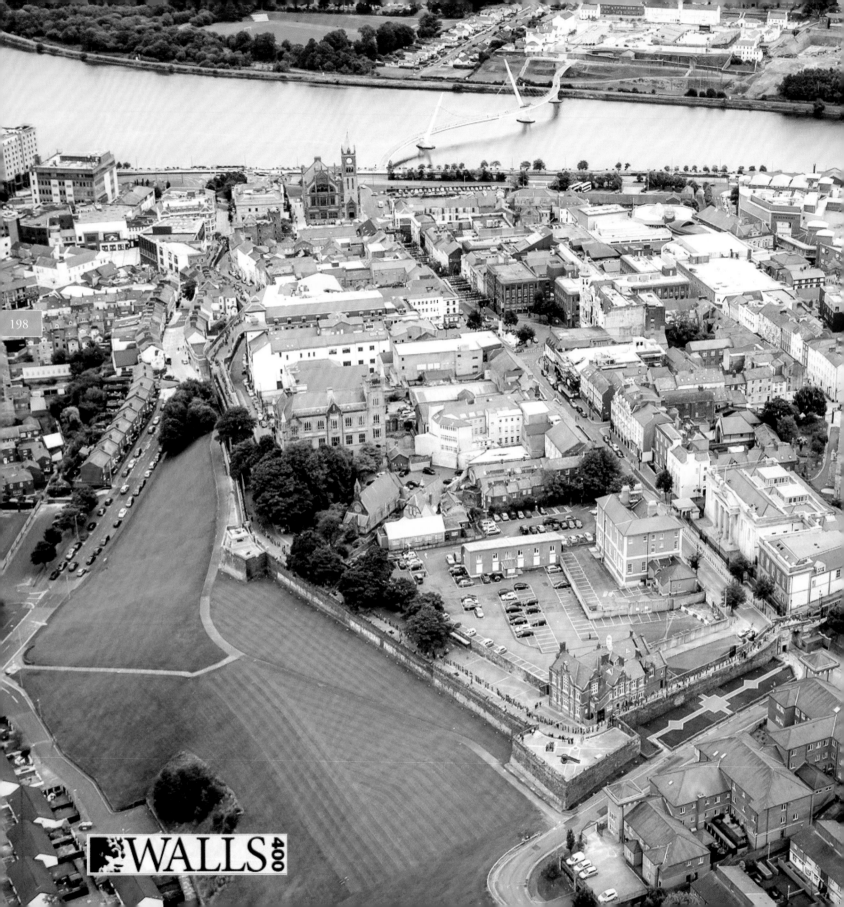

WALLS400

Above: Seána, Ronin and Holly Hippsley are among the participants enjoying Derry Walls Day 2013.

Left: Derry Walls Day – part of the Walls400 celebrations. The line of 1,950 people in red 'Wave on the Walls' T-shirts makes the city walls clearly visible from above. The perimeter of Derry's walls was first marked out in August 1613 by representatives from the City of London. That simple act, four centuries ago, has left us a tremendous physical legacy in the form of the largest ancient monument in the North. On Derry Walls Day, this mile-long 'Mexican Wave', created by a very diverse group of volunteers, affirms that, 400 years on, these historic ramparts belong to everyone. © Rory O'Doherty.

200

(Photograph © Rory O'Doherty)

Left: An amazing image of the line of volunteers from Church Bastion to Artillery Bastion, just some of the 1,950 people creating a continuous red line around Derry's ramparts as part of Derry Walls Day 2013. Participants completed three 'Mexican Waves' along the full one-mile circuit of the walls. Each wave was started in turn by Mayor Martin Reilly, Rev Dr William Morton, Dean of St Columb's Cathedral and Martin McGuinness, Deputy First Minister. They were joined by living-history performers (above) representing the London, Scottish and Irish people who would have been in Derry in 1613. The 'Wave on the Walls' event was followed by a 1613 Charter Market transporting Guildhall Square back to its life 400 years ago as Derry's Ship Quay. Derry Walls Day was part of National Heritage Week and was organised by Holywell Trust's City Walls Heritage Project.

WALLED CITY TATTOO

Above: DETI Minister Arlene Foster (above and below in red) visits Ebrington for the launch of the Walled City Tattoo. © Martin McKeown, courtesy Culture Company.

There is something about a Tattoo, it doesn't matter if it's raining or anything else, the music makes the hair stand up on the back of your neck.

Georgina Kee, WCT organiser

MPs Gregory Campbell and Kate Hoey with Mayor Martin Reilly and performers at the Walled City Tattoo. © Tom Heaney.

Shona McCarthy, Martin Reilly, Martin McGuinness and Carál Ní Chuilín at the opening of the Walled City Tattoo. © Tom Heaney.

Scenes from Derry's history as performed at the Walled City Tattoo. Courtesy Culture Company.

The Foyle Pride 20th Anniversary parade reaches the Guildhall. © Anna Czajak.

Free Derry Wall goes pink for Pride. Courtesy Culture Company.

Scenes from the Foyle Pride parade. Courtesy Culture Company.

Foyle Pride. Courtesy Culture Company.

The Guildhall clock face is turned pink for the day.

A rainbow of colour lights up Shipquay Street. © Anna Czajak.

Young artists taking part in the Xchange Project at the Playhouse. © Gavan Connolly.

Motion Ensemble at Echo Echo studios. © Sarah Bryden, courtesy Echo Echo.

music for a new revolution

A weekend of political and topical song across the city features contributions from Billy Bragg, Teknopeasant, Connor Kelly, Conor McAteer, Paddy Nash & the Happy Enchiladas, Steve White and the Protest Family, Robb Johnston, Colm Bryce, Jinx Lennon, The Wood Burning Savages, Eamon Friel and Little Hooks. © Gavan Connolly.

Walker's Plinth is opened to the public to mark European Heritage Open Days. It's the first time the landmark (inset) on the city walls is accessible in the 40 years since the pillar was blown up in 1973. Courtesy Mark Lusby.

the memory of the

Seamus Heaney's death had a profound impact, not just in Derry but nationally and internationally. Locally, a special St Columb's College celebration of the poet's life at St Columb's Hall on September 19 – which had been due to feature both the poet and Snow Patrol – was cancelled.

Some of the biggest names from Channel 4's hit TV show 'Hollyoaks' filmed a storyline in Derry in September, courtesy of the show's producer, and Culture Company mentor, Phil Redmond. The filmmakers captured many of the city's iconic landmarks and locations during their shoot, which focused on a sham marriage. Filming took place at the Peace Bridge, Guildhall Square, Waterloo Place, the city walls, Shipquay Street, inside the Guildhall and on Spencer Road in the Waterside. The featured episodes were screened in November.

The work of the Derry-born artist, the late Eamonn O'Doherty, was celebrated in The London Street Gallery during September in an exhibition entitled 'A Man for All Mediums'. A successful campaign subsequently sprang up to keep O'Doherty's Armoured Pram as a sculpture for the city.

The twice Turner-nominated Derry artist Willie Doherty also launched a major retrospective in September. 'Unseen', which was curated by Pearse Moore at the City Factory, included photographs and video installations.

The highlight of the year for techies, gamers and digital enthusiasts was undoubtedly the week-long CultureTech Festival which featured more than 150 sessions and 500 speakers. The festival included a substantial music element, too, with performances from Jetplane Landing, Utah Saints and Axis Of.

Derry rock legends Fighting With Wire organised and headlined the 'Cut the Transmission' showcase in The Venue at the end of September with Making Monsters, Droids, Little Hooks, Jim Lockey & the Solemn Sun, Frank Turner and The Sleeping Souls, More than Conquerors and LaFaro.

And theatre critics from all over the globe assembled at Ebrington Square on September 24 for the world premiere of Haris Pasovic's 'promenade' drama 'The Conquest of Happiness'. The *Financial Times* described the piece as 'a powerful, unremitting portrayal of division and conflict'.

Little Hooks on stage at 'Cut the Transmission', Fighting with Wire's (below) farewell rockfest. © Gavan Connolly.

Above: Archaeologists uncover 13 skeletons while digging in the carpark adjacent to the city's oldest church, St Augustine's, on the city walls. Courtesy Mark Lusby.

Above right: Jenni Doherty, winner of the inaugural Noelle Vail Tyrone Guthrie Poetry Bursary Award for her debut poetry collection 'Rain Spill', published by Guildhall Press. Courtesy Derry Journal.

Right: Filmmaker and photographer Vincent O'Callaghan at the opening of an exhibition of his work at Eden Place Arts Centre, Pilot's Row.

Men with a dream: The year 2013 marked 50 years since Martin Luther King delivered his inspirational 'I have a dream' oration – indeed, his son would visit the city during the year to talk about the speech's ongoing significance. (He is pictured here behind the scenes at the City Hotel with City of Culture ambassador Chris McMonagle.) In the autumn, Derry's Peace Laureate John Hume – a winner of the Martin Luther King Peace Prize – is invited by the BBC to recite a section of the speech for broadcast on Radio 4. Courtesy Culture Company.

Culture**TECH**

CultureTech – Derry's annual celebration of digital technology, music and media – records its most successful year to date.

Pictured here are participants enjoying a range of workshops and music events from performers/DJs such as Kwa Daniels (Bounce) and Utah Saints. Courtesy Mark Nagurski, CultureTech.

212

Portstewart band Axis Of perform live at CultureTech.

Portrait of a City display images on the city walls as part of CultureTech.

213

Maggie Philbin from Teen Tech with Aela Stewart, Orla McGeogh and Eimear Watson from Brookbridge Primary School at the BBC NI stand at CultureTech. © Carrie Davenport.

SYNC Music Promise

The biggest single community programme of 2013 was the Sync Music Promise initiative, which engaged more than 1,000 young people across the city in music creation, collaboration and, importantly, performance. The initiative, which was run by the Nerve Centre, saw training and mentoring sessions take place four nights a week in every neighbourhood of the city. There were scores of public performances, too – many facilitated by 2013 Musician-in-Residence Neil Cowley (Adele's pianist), pictured far right at Pilot's Row with Cormac Clarke, Stephanie Toland and Deirbhile McSheffrey. © Martin McKeown. The Sync Music Promise proved so successful that it is now in line for long-term funding as a legacy project. Dozens of visiting international musicians, such as the legendary guitar virtuoso Steve Vai (above), took part in the project, tutoring and playing alongside young Derry musicians. © Lorcan Doherty.

Left: International footballer Tony O'Doherty and champion boxer Charlie Nash are hosted by BBC journalist Richie Kelly at a special night of Creggan sporting memories at the Hive Studio, Ráth Mór.

Right: Charlie and Tony are joined in the line-up by Conal McFeely of Creggan Enterprises.

Media blitz: there was huge media interest in the events of 2013. The BBC's input and coverage – which included keynote events such as Sons and Daughters and One Big Weekend – was valued at more than £100m in marketing terms for the city. Johnston Press, via the their two city flagships, the Derry Journal and the Londonderry Sentinel, were the City of Culture's official Print Media Partners. They produced a top-quality, monthly '2013' magazine, and promoted the year, and its events, in 300 JP titles across the islands. Throughout the year, the city played host to journalists from all over the world – from the New York Times to the Sydney Herald – and invariably the reaction was positive. UTV also invested heavily in their programming, with Joe Mahon (right, interviewing author Garbhan Downey) producing 12 hour-long specials from Derry in a series called 'Lesser Spotted Culture'. Joe Mahon is pictured above on location on the banks of the Foyle with his Westway Productions crew, comprising Billy Gallagher, Patrick Mahon, Orlagh Bann and Vinny Cunningham. © Lorcan Doherty.

Enjoying a tea-break here is Stephen Bradley, star of 'By Mr Farquhar', which tells the story of the Derry-born 17th-century playwright, who became one of the biggest names in British theatre. Stephen is pictured in Cafe Soul on Guildhall Square, shortly before appearing on the Mark Patterson show to have his head shaved – live on air – for the part. 'By Mr Farquhar', written by Lindsay Sedgwick and directed by Caroline Byrne, is one of a series of theatrical events from Jonathan Burgess's Blue Eagle Theatre Company, dedicated to celebrating the life and work of George Farquhar and showcased at the Waterside Theatre.

Left: Scenes from 'The Conquest of Happiness', a huge outdoor performance drama, directed by Haris Pasovic (bottom left) and staged at Ebrington Square. Included in images are: Dermott Hickson, who plays Bloody Sunday victim Jackie Duddy, Mona Muratovic, Thomas Steyaert playing Victor Jara, Shane O'Reilly, Matt Faris and Cornelius Macarthy as Bertrand Russell. Courtesy Culture Company.

Right: The New York launch of Derry author Desmond Doherty's debut novel 'Valberg', published by Guildhall Press. Des Doherty is pictured here with The Mysterious Bookshop's Ian Kern.

The cast of 'Hollyoaks' arrive at the City Hotel, Derry. Included are: Claire McDermott (Culture Company), John Omolen (Vincent), Lucy Dickson (Tilly), Mandip Gill (Phoebe), Tony McDaid (Translink), Jasmine Franks (Esther) and Steven Roberts (George).
© Martin McKeown, courtesy Culture Company.

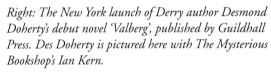

The work of Derry-born artist Eamonn O'Doherty is celebrated in the London Street Gallery during September in an exhibition entitled 'A Man for All Mediums'. Pictured at the opening of the exhibition (top right) are: Mrs Barbara O'Doherty, Mark Durkan MP, Alderman Gary Middleton, Deputy Mayor, and Noelle McAlinden. Courtesy Culture Company.

Also attending the London Street Gallery exhibition launch are Eoin O'Doherty with a portrait of himself painted by his late father; the artist's daughter Megan and his son Eoin with the sculpture Pegasus; and Barbara O'Doherty with her late husband's sculpture, Minerva.

Above: Noelle McAlinden and Martin Melarkey with the work Armoured Pram. Featured above and left are 'Save the Pram' campaigners, including Michael Bradley, Steve Jones and Gary Middleton. Pictured on right is two-year-old Gray Osborn from Northland Road. Courtesy Culture Company.

WILLIE DOHERTY 'UNSEEN' AT THE CITY FACTORY

Pictures from the launch of two-time Turner nominee Willie Doherty's landmark new exhibition 'Unseen' featuring photographic and video installations. Included are: Brendan McMenamin, Shona McCarthy, Pearse Moore, Gareth Stewart, Brian Fisher and (right) Willie Doherty.

Derry participants in the global 'Thrill the World' zombie flash mob — simulating a mass performance of Michael Jackson's Thriller dance.
© Gavan Connolly.

Any thoughts of a lull in proceedings were vanquished by the imminent arrival in the city of the Turner Prize, Europe's most prestigious modern-art competition. The entire Ebrington site was transformed in preparation for the red-carpet opening ceremony on October 22.

The nominated artists arrived to inspect their installations and were delighted with the new gallery – regenerated from 19th-century military dorms.

There was also some (mostly tongue-in-cheek) media controversy surrounding David Shrigley's nude model, which led to cautious warnings being issued to school groups.

On the drama front, The Royal Shakespeare Company arrived at the Waterside Theatre to stage the narrative poem 'The Rape of Lucrece', as performed by Camille O'Sullivan and directed by Elizabeth Freestone. The score for the production was co-written by the Derry composer Feargal Murray.

Elsewhere, the Derry troupe An Nua staged 'Derry 24' – a history of the city over the course of a day – at the Playhouse; while ex-pat director Andy Hinds returned home to premiere his new play 'Sea Lavender', set during the Siege of Derry.

The musical mayhem continued along merrily, with thousands of choristers of all ages descending from across Europe for the City of Derry International Choir Festival. There was an October Metal Fest at The Venue. And a host of local musicians – including Paddy Nash & the Happy Enchiladas, John Deery, Declan McLaughlin, Tracy Cullen, Jeanette Hutton, Eamon Friel, Little Hooks and Teknopeasant – launched their 'Six Strings & Stigma' album to raise awareness of mental-health issues.

And there was visual art aplenty away from Ebrington, too – with the 'No Jury, No Prize' exhibition in the London Street Gallery and Locky Morris's installation above a Creggan barber shop.

Above: Artwork by James Cunningham, commissioned by Culture Company, merging quotes taken from a series of interviews with older residents of the city with images captured by James during the year.

Opposite: 'Derry 24', an innovative theatre piece from An Nua, features dozens of artists from throughout the Northwest giving their alternative portrait of the city. The piece combines strong characters, puppeteering, innovative design and music by Lorna McLaughlin of the Henry Girls, Gay McIntyre, and Martin Coyle from Balkan Alien Sound.

One of the new community initiatives supported by DCAL programme funding is a pilot digital radio station, Hive Studios FM, pictured here broadcasting from Ráth Mór. Presenter Paul McFadden is shown above with producer Eimear O'Callaghan, audio engineer Ciaran Downey and guests Amie Gallagher, Carol Cunningham and Julieann Campbell. Other guests on 'McFadden Online' include (below) Martine Mulhern, William Allen and Martin McCrossan, and (bottom) Denis Bradley, Brian Dougherty and Michael Doherty.

A WEEK IN GOALS

An installation by Derry artist Locky Morris, situated in the heart of the community where he grew up, at the Beechwood Shops in Creggan. Courtesy Culture Company.

Writers' Corner

Above left: Writers on the radio – Resonance 104.4FM broadcasts live from Little Acorns Bookstore. Featured are Guildhall Press authors Charlie Herron, Dave Duggan, Freya McClements and Desmond Doherty. Above centre: Filmmaker Raymond Craig and author Hazel Philson are interviewed about their latest works. Above right: Poet, novelist and critic Nick Laird pops into Little Acorns Bookstore on a visit to Derry to promote his latest collection of poetry, 'Go Giants'. Courtesy Jenni Doherty and Grainne McCool.

Right: Mayor Martin Reilly with Poet Laureate Carol Ann Duffy during her visit to the city. Also included: Jenni Doherty (Guildhall Press), Iain Barr (Waterside Theatre), Claire McDermott (Culture Company), John Sampson (musician), and Eamonn Baker (Yes! Publications).

Far right: Musician John Sampson with Poet Laureate Carol Ann Duffy at their performance in the Waterside Theatre organised by Yes! Publications and Guildhall Press.

Above and below: Theatre of Witness 'Sanctuary' workshop at the Playhouse.
© Gavan Connolly.

Above and below: Scenes from the Royal Shakespeare Company's adaptation of the Bard's epic poem 'The Rape of Lucrece' at the Waterside Theatre. The performance is doubly significant, as the score was co-created by Derry native Feargal Murray with his long-time collaborator Camille O'Sullivan.

Sacred Heart PS Choir.

Holy Family PS Choir.

CITY OF DERRY INTERNATIONAL CHORAL FESTIVAL

Chapel Road PS Choir.

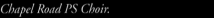
Below: Lisnagelvin PS Choir.

Nazareth House PS Choir.

Below: St Cecilia's College Choir.

Thornhill College Choir.

St Mary's College Choir.

The City of Derry International Choral Festival showcases fantastic choirs from local schools, national and international choirs who are invited to take part in a range of competitions. Images © Lorcan Doherty, courtesy Walled City Music Festival.

Concert pianist Ruth McGinley.

City Song host Mark Patterson.

St Columb's College Choir.

Lumen Christi College Choir.

Below: Winning international choir Voci Nuove with the Adjudication Panel and Artistic Director of the festival, Dónal Doherty.

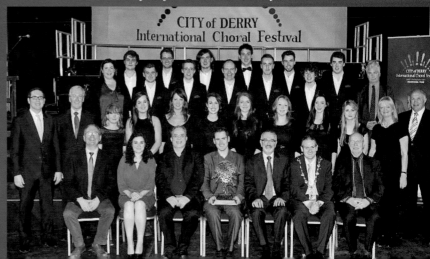

CITY of DERRY
International Choral Festival

BANKS OF THE FOYLE
HALLOWEEN CARNIVAL

© GC

© AM

*A parade of phantoms, more
than 20,000 strong, haunts
Derry's streets at Halloween.
© Gavan Connolly, Andrea
Mitchell and Simon Fallaha.*

© GC

© GC

227

© AM

© AM

© AM

© AM

© SF

Inferno: A theatrical other-world of light, fire and circus erupts on the city streets at Halloween. © Anna Czajak.

Getting her teeth into the part: Claire Harrigan and her family of gory zombies take part in the global Thriller-inspired flash mob. © Gavan Connolly.

The Dean of St Columb's Cathedral, Very Rev Dr William Morton, hosts an evening reception for the European Walled Towns Symposium 2013. Dean Morton, centre, is pictured with some of the delegates from the 32 walled towns from 13 countries attending the event organised by Holywell Trust's City Walls Heritage Project and Derry City Council. Courtesy Mark Lusby.

NO STIGMA HERE

Dozens of Derry musicians take part in the production and recording of a new album targeting the stigma of suicide. 'Six Strings & Stigma' features tracks from Paddy Nash & the Happy Enchiladas, Teknopeasant, Intermission, Little Hooks, Declan McLaughlin, Ard Rí, Wood Burning Savages, Murder Balladeers, Tara Gi, The Gatefolds, We Are Aerials, John Deery and the Heads, Jeanette Hutton, Rory Donaghy, and Tracy Cullen. Courtesy Culture Company.

TURNER GALLERY OPENS AT EBRINGTON

The Turner Prize, the world's most prestigious art competition and a City of Culture keynote event, opens at a purpose-built gallery at Ebrington. Tens of thousands flock to view work from artists Laure Prouvost, Tino Sehgal, David Shrigley and Lynette Yiadom-Boakye.

Right: Artist David Shrigley in a tactful pose in front of his 'controversial' sculpture.

Below: The new gallery space at Ebrington; and (right), three of the shortlisted artists visit the Turner gallery for the first time.

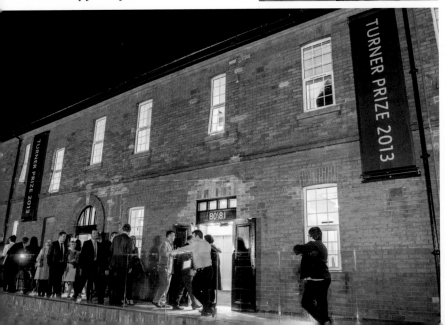

A section of Laure Prouvost's installation.

Part of Lynette Yiadom-Boakye's entry.

Below: Turner artists Laure Prouvost, David Shrigley and Lynette Yiadom-Boakye pictured at Ebrington. © Martin McKeown, courtesy Culture Company.

233

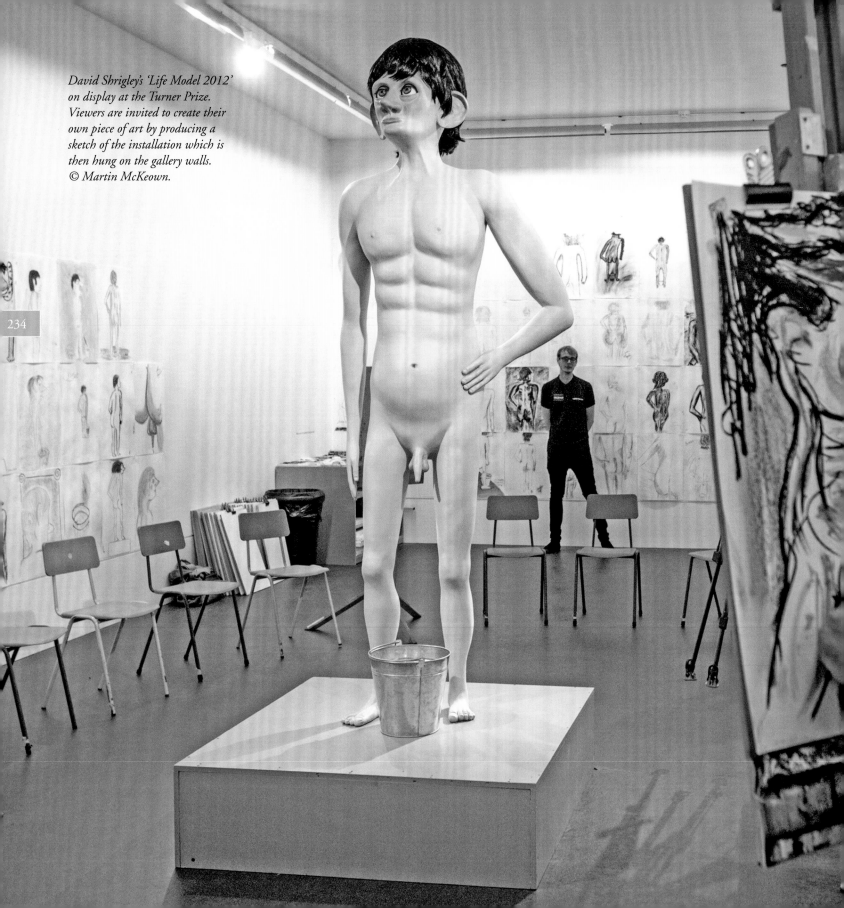

234

David Shrigley's 'Life Model 2012'
on display at the Turner Prize.
Viewers are invited to create their
own piece of art by producing a
sketch of the installation which is
then hung on the gallery walls.
© Martin McKeown.

Above: Barbara Johns, British-Irish Secretariat, and Roisin McDonough, Arts Council NI, at the Turner launch.

Below: Lisa and Robert Scott pictured at the reception for the opening of the Turner Prize. Robert Scott's father William painted the original artwork in Altnagelvin Hospital. © Martin McKeown, courtesy Culture Company.

Guests at the Turner opening include: Peter Johnston, Susan Lovell, Larry Deeney and Richard Yarr, Bronagh and Chris McCann, Mr & Mrs Andrew Potter, Aine Gallagher and Claire McDermott, Donal O'Doherty, Oonagh McGillion, John and Fiona McCandless, Jacqueline McIntyre, Grainne Devine, David Thomas, Shona McCarthy and Graeme Farrow, Joe Mahon, Mark and Deirdre Lusby, Patricia and Roy Devine, John Pollock, Margaret Ann O'Sullivan, Ian Morrison, Emmett McCourt, Simon Duggan, Odhran Dunne, Richard O'Rawe, Sinead and Fergal McNicholl, Mo Durkan, April Garfield-Kidd, Prof Richard Barnett, Dr Aideen McGinley, Eamonn McCann and Goretti Horgan. © Martin McKeown, courtesy Culture Company.

Derry writers address a session of the Women of the World Festival at the Playhouse. The event – organised by the Southbank Centre in partnership with Culture Company – includes debates, workshops, music, comedy and performance celebrating the achievements of women and exploring the issues they face. © Emmett McLaughlin.

November

As the nights got darker, the summer levity was soon swapped for murder most foul, not in the literal sense but rather the *literary* sense, with the staging of the first annual Killer Books Festival at the Verbal Arts Centre. Top crime authors Lee Child, Colin Bateman (whose punk musical 'Teenage Kicks' was opening in Derry the same weekend), Des Doherty and a host of others took part in a series of readings and discussions curated by Derry's own thriller supremo, Brian McGilloway.

The darker side of art was also to be savoured in Field Day's final offering of the year – the international premiere of the blood-spattered, Oedipal drama 'A Particle of Dread'.

But by the end of the month, the skies would brighten again; brighten hugely, in fact, with the launch of the Lumiere International Festival of Light produced by the Artichoke Trust. Landmarks across the city – bridges, walls and factories – were transformed with neon signs, lights and sculptures (or, in the case of St Columb's Park, live flames).

November was also Cinema City month, and a litany of top Hollywood names – including Danny Boyle, Sam Shepard and Paul Greengrass – visited Derry to introduce films and host discussions with audiences.

The penultimate month of 2013 also saw the Southbank Centre host their annual Women of the World Festival at the Playhouse. The event, which celebrates the achievements of women and discusses the obstacles they have to face across the world, had never been held in Ireland before. It featured contributions from many city cultural leaders including Margo Harkin, Jenni Doherty, Freya McClements, Anita Robinson, Mary Murphy, Finola Deane and Shona McCarthy.

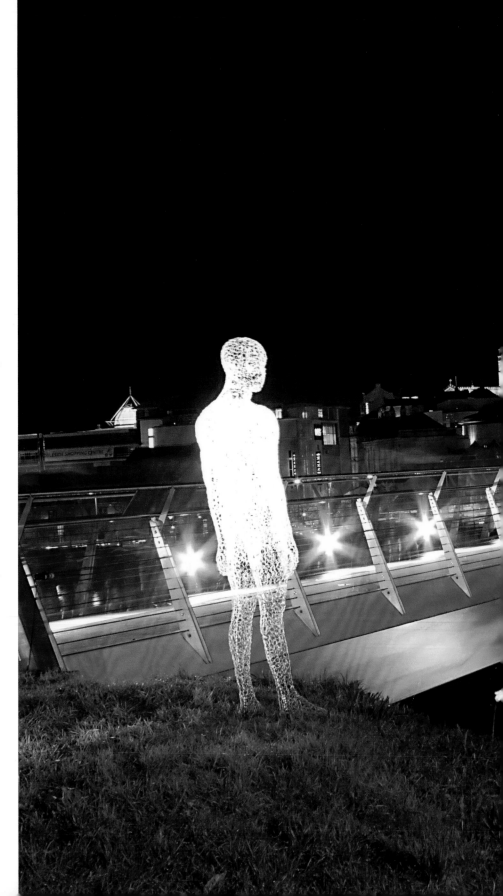

The city is illuminated as never before for the Artichoke Trust's Lumiere International Festival of Light. © John Boyle.

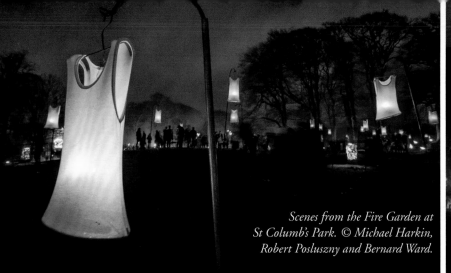

Scenes from the Fire Garden at St Columb's Park. © Michael Harkin, Robert Posluszny and Bernard Ward.

*Awe and wonder at the
Fire Garden in St Columb's
Park © Michael Harkin.*

Dreamlike scenes from the Fire Garden at St Columb's Park © Stephen Boyle and Michael Harkin.

LUMIERE

The Clocktower building at Ebrington is the backdrop for a series of animated projections created by local schoolchildren. © Stephen Boyle.

Buildings will change their shape and appearance; human forms will seem to fly through the air, parks and empty public spaces will become places where strange and delightful things happen.

Helen Marriage
Artistic Director, Lumiere Festival

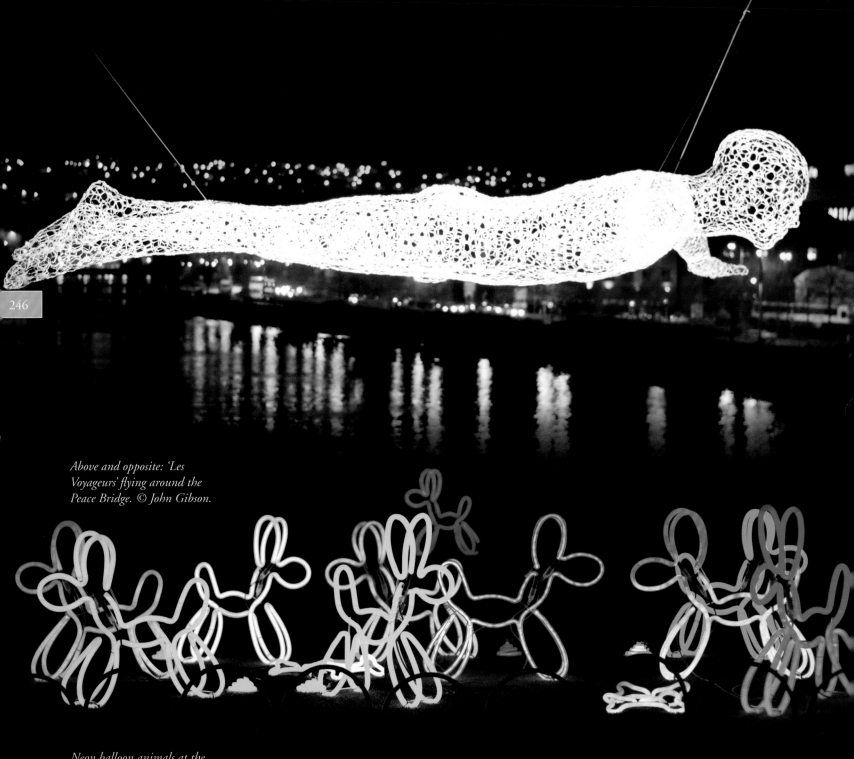

Above and opposite: 'Les Voyageurs' flying around the Peace Bridge. © John Gibson.

Neon balloon animals at the Apprentice Boys' Memorial Hall. © Brendan McMenamin.

*The hi-tec projection centre
at Ebrington Square.
© Brendan McMenamin.*

A spectacular light show on the world's oldest department store – Austins of the Diamond. © Brendan McMenamin.

The 'Empty Plinth' on the city walls lights up for Lumiere. © Mark Lusby.

248

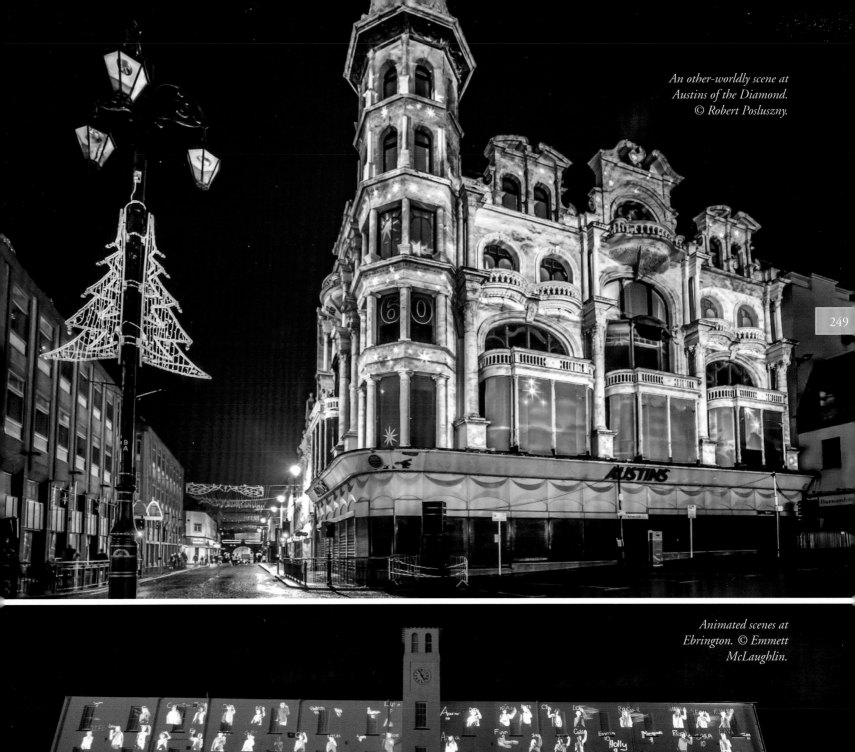

An other-worldly scene at Austins of the Diamond. © Robert Posluszny.

Animated scenes at Ebrington. © Emmett McLaughlin.

As part of Cinema City, the LSO perform the score from 'Psycho' at a live screening of the classic film at The Venue.
© Lorcan Doherty.

Foyle Film Festival and Cinema City showcase 'An Evening with Danny Boyle and Frank Cottrell Boyce' at St Columb's Hall.
© Lorcan Doherty.

Martin Melarkey and Shauna Kelpie with film legend Sam Shepard at the Brunswick Moviebowl. © Lorcan Doherty.

Guildhall Press author Dave Duggan shares a joke with actor, writer and director Sam Shepard. © Gavan Connolly.

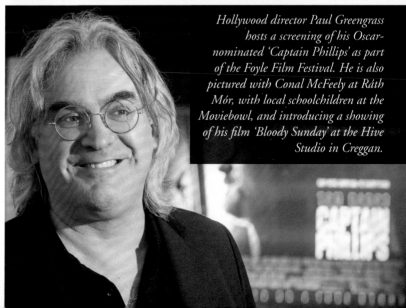

Hollywood director Paul Greengrass hosts a screening of his Oscar-nominated 'Captain Phillips' as part of the Foyle Film Festival. He is also pictured with Conal McFeely at Ráth Mór, with local schoolchildren at the Moviebowl, and introducing a showing of his film 'Bloody Sunday' at the Hive Studio in Creggan.

Equinox jazz night at the Guildhall featuring Gay McIntyre. © Gavan Connolly.

Pictured below with the BBC's Eve Blair are Paul McGuckin and Andrew Horsman of Landscape Ireland. Paul and Andrew photographed a series of Derry scenes using a replica 19th-century camera, and merged these new modern-day images with archive originals from 100 years ago to create large-scale artworks which are now on public display at Ebrington Square (pictured opposite). Courtesy Landscape Ireland.

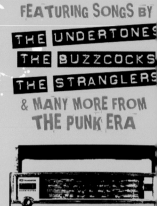

Award-winning author Colin Bateman adds a new string to his bow by penning a punk musical celebrating his misspent youth. Produced by the Nerve Centre, 'Teenage Kicks' is a tale of lust and love set in the 1970s featuring music from some of the era's top bands including The Undertones. Above left: Cast members Ben Kerr, Mikey-Jay Heath and Keith Lynch join Colin Bateman and Deputy Mayor Gary Middleton for a spot of pre-premiere pogoing. Left: The cast of Teenage Kicks take to the stage to a warm reception at the Millennium Forum. Courtesy Nerve Centre.

Below left: The first highlight of the Playhouse's dramatic offerings for November is 'The Clearing', a powerful drama of love, passion, treachery and tragedy set in 17th-century Ireland. The play features critically acclaimed performances from Kieran Griffiths and Megan Armitage. © Gavan Connolly.

Below: Danny Boyle takes a break from the film circuit to sketch David Shrigley's sculpture at the Turner Gallery in Ebrington while Brian Quinn gives him some artistic advice. Courtesy Culture Company.

November's Killer Books Festival sees some of the world's top crime writers descend on Derry. Courtesy Culture Company.

Love your book (above): the internationally renowned thriller writer Lee Child, in Derry for the Killer Books Festival, swaps one of his bestsellers for Desmond Doherty's debut novel 'Valberg'.

Left: A section of the large crowd congregated inside First Derry Presbyterian Church for Brian McGilloway's interview with Lee Child. Courtesy Culture Company.

International bestsellers (below left): Killer Books Festival organiser Brian McGilloway with headline guest Lee Child at the Verbal Arts Centre. Courtesy Culture Company.

Right: Oscar-winning songwriter Glen Hansard pictured during an intimate gig at Cool Discs independent record shop on Foyle Street. Waiting for autographs after the show are Fiacre Gaffney, Lee Mason and Mark Burns.

All good clean fun: Field Day's production of the new Sam Shepard play 'A Particle of Dread' at the Playhouse wins rave reviews – though it is not for the squeamish. The play stars Stephen Rea and Judith Roddy and is directed by Nancy Meckler. © Ros Kavanagh, courtesy the Playhouse.

Derry has now seen beyond the war. Think of Derry as a child with a new voice. A place of thousands of nests with wee eggs about to hatch.

Bronagh Gallagher

Portraying a City

One of the year's major success stories was the Portrait of a City project, based at the Hive Studio at Ráth Mór. A team of archivists, led by Kirsty Osborn, Jim Collins, Emmett McLaughlin, Terence Coyle, Harriet Purkis and Declan Sheehan; with technical support by Guildhall Press began compiling and curating a massive database of community photographs, film and video, with the aim of developing a digital 'memory bank' of Derry. Their finds include some priceless private collections, which have sparked exhibitions and showcases across the city's communities and also nationally and internationally. The flagship project won a prestigious gong when it was voted Digital Culture Project of the Year at the 2013 Digital Advertising NI awards. Long-term, the archive, which is being continually upgraded and developed by Guildhall Press and the POAC team, will be used as a tourism and genealogical resource. Images © Emmett McLaughlin.

Women of the World Festival

Factory Girls' Reunion

with Margaret Crabtree

3pm – 4pm

Women from all over the city take part in the Southbank Centre's festival at the Playhouse, celebrating the achievements of women across the globe. Included in images are: Kathryn Ferguson, Gabrielle Tierney, Shona McCarthy, Margo Harkin, Megan McClean, Anita Robinson, Freya McClements, Mary Doherty, Bridie McIntyre, Beverley Caldwell, Clare Cregan, Margaret Cassidy, Claire McDermott, Jenni Doherty, Domino Pateman, Sue Bourne, Sue Kreitzman, Helen Faulkner, Helena Zedig, Julia Evans, Edel Dunlop, Pauline Leckey, Teresa Lafferty, Mary Logue, Bridget Concannon and Anne Gallagher. © Martin McKeown, courtesy Culture Company.

Some of Derry's best-known landmarks, including the Rosemount Factory and the Artillery Street Playhouse, are illuminated for the closing night of Lumiere. © Bernard Ward.

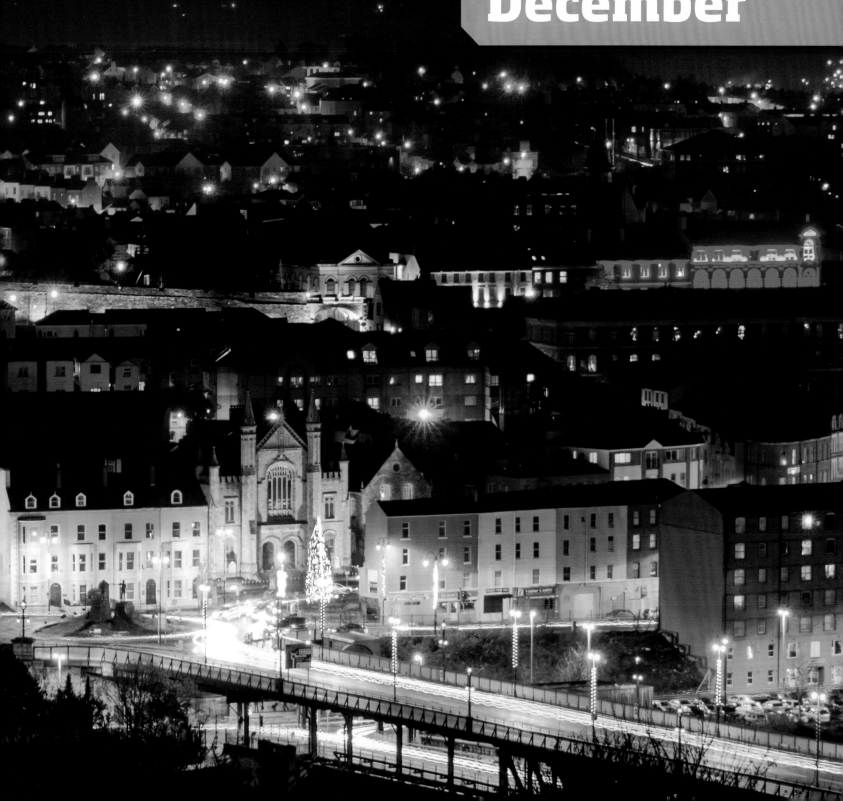

December

Tens of thousands of winter tourists flooded into the city for the conclusion of the Lumiere Festival at the start of December, delighted at the news that the St Columb's Park Fire Garden would be retained for an extra night. Indeed, the *Derry Journal* put the visitor count for the four-day spectacle at 180,000!

December 2 witnessed one of the biggest media events of the year with the announcement of the Turner Prize winner. The £25,000 prize – Europe's top modern-art gong – was won by the French-born installation artist Laure Prouvost. The award was presented by the actress Saoirse Ronan, and the event was broadcast live on Channel 4.

The run-in to Christmas saw a series of book and DVD launches, including: Emmett McCourt's epic culinary history of the Northwest, 'Feast or Famine'; the second volume of Sean McLaughlin's 'Lost Archives' series; Raymond Craig's documentary 'The Saint & The Soldier'; Catherine Canning's poetry collection 'Inch Days'; and the London launch of Des Doherty's crime-thriller 'Valberg', hosted by the eminent barrister Michael Mansfield.

Drama fans got to witness three new monologues written by the award-winning Derry author Jennifer Johnston. Performances were held both at the Playhouse and at three 'secret' locations – including the now derelict Boom Hall.

The year's official finale took place on December 20, in the form of a stunning re-enactment of Shaun Davey's Relief of Derry symphony at The Venue. The piece – featuring 220 on-stage musicians including Liam Óg O'Flynn, Gerard McChrystal, Liam Ó Maonlaí, the full Ulster Orchestra and a marching band – had originally been commissioned by Kevin McCaul of Derry City Council and was first performed in Derry in 1990.

In all, from the opening tea dance, the city had witnessed more than 500 cultural events, ranging from community exhibitions to massive international showcases. We welcomed hundreds of thousands of new visitors and established the region, once and for all, as a cultural jewel on the international map.

Neil Cowley, 2013 Musician-in-Residence, summed up the year perfectly when he wrote: "It's lyrical and wonderful and beautiful, and it has been amazing to be a part of."

A colourful Craft Village at the conclusion of the Lumiere Festival. © Bernard Ward.

A neon forest springs up in the Craft Village. © Robert Posluszny.

A STITCH IN TIME

Rosemount Factory celebrates its shirt-making heritage.

A giant light installation at Abbey Street. © Anna Czajak.

© Phil Cunningham.

© Anna Czajak.

Ronin Hippsley in
the hot seat!

Closing Scenes From Lumiere

265

© Robert Posluszny.

© (Left & below) Andrea Mitchell.

© Deirdre Harte.

Above: Scenes from Jennifer Johnston's 'Three Monologues' performed on location at Boom Hall and at the Playhouse. © Gavan Connolly.

Above left: Hothouse Flowers' frontman Liam Ó Maonlaí is presented with a copy of Guildhall Press's 'City of Music' by fellow musician Declan Carlin during a recording session at the Blast Furnace studio in Ráth Mór.

Left: Sustrans open the new bike trail lapping the city. © Gavan Connolly.

Right: Artist Locky Morris beside 'Dead On', a new piece of public art created from a dead elm tree in Brooke Park. © Gavan Connolly.

Below left: Catherine Canning pictured at the Playhouse with her family, celebrating the launch of 'Inch Days', her debut collection of poetry and paintings.

Below right: Making pots at a workshop in Eden Place Arts Centre, Pilot's Row. Included are Kathleen Logue and Aileen McManus. © Judi Logue.

A Taste of Derry

A capacity crowd pack into the City Hotel for the year's biggest book launch and cookery demonstration. 'Feast or Famine' by the award-winning chef Emmett McCourt celebrates the city's rich culinary heritage and worldwide reach. Images © Stephen Boyle.

Above: Emmett McCourt with proud parents Denis and Angela at the launch of 'Feast or Famine'.

Above right: Emmett McCourt and family – Mary, Danaé, Luke and Georgia.

Right: Kevin Hippsley and Jenni Doherty, Guildhall Press, Emmett McCourt and sponsor Conal McFeely, Creggan Enterprises.

Below left: Supporters Brenda Stevenson and Mary Blake with the author at the launch in the City Hotel.

Below right: Deputy First Minister Martin McGuinness, who contributed a recipe for the publication, congratulates the author.

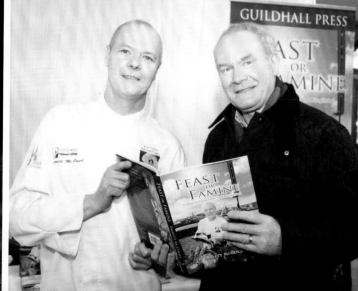

And the winner is ... judges' favourite Laure Prouvost is congratulated by Saoirse Ronan, Master of Ceremonies for the Turner Prize.

Opposite: Images from the Turner ceremony at The Venue. Included in shots are: Shona McCarthy, host, Martin Melarkey, Carál Ní Chuilín, Martin and Amanda Bradley, Teresa Villiers, Fiona Kane, Joe Connolly, Pauline Ross, Aoife Nic an tSaoir, Geraldine McAteer, Noelle McAlinden, Bridie Mullin, Paddy Mackey, Gavin Killeen, Margaret-Ann O'Sullivan, Ian Morrison and Emmett McCourt. © Martin McKeown, courtesy Culture Company.

This year the Turner Prize is presented by Derry~Londonderry, the UK's first City of Culture, in partnership with Tate.

LOUGH FOYLE IRISH FLAT OYSTER

Above: Michael Mansfield QC (host) and Baroness Doreen Lawrence, pictured with author Desmond Doherty at the London launch of his thriller 'Valberg'.

Below: More than 200 musicians take to the stage for Shaun Davey's 'Relief of Derry' symphony at The Venue. Included here are piper Liam Óg O'Flynn, Rita Connolly, and composer Shaun Davey with the city's long-time cultural champion Kevin McCaul and wife Maisie. Courtesy Culture Company.

Right: Raymond Craig launches his documentary 'The Saint & The Soldier' at the Hive Studio at Ráth Mór.

Above right: 'Derry Journal Lost Archives' compiler Sean McLaughlin (second from right) pictured with fellow Journal staff at the official launch. Front from left: Martin McGinley, Pat McArt and Mary McLaughlin. Back from left: John Conway, Margaret Foley, Theresa Casey, David Wilson, Michael McMonagle, Julieann Campbell and Mary McGuire. © Jim McCafferty.

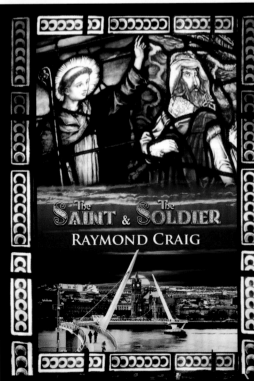

Shipquay Street is shrouded in a blanket of lights for Christmas.
© Brendan McMenamin.

Sea change: a fiery farewell to a LegenDerry year. Pyrotechnics light up the sky for New Year's Eve in celebration of the city's cultural, artistic and community achievements in 2013.
© *Stephen Boyle.*